CRIMINAL**PROFILE**

INTO THE MIND OF THE KILLER

CRIMINALPROFILE
INTO THE MIND OF THE KILLER

Wayne Petherick
Foreword by Val McDermid
Introduction by Brent Turvey

modern
books

Published by Modern Books
79 St John St
London EC1M 4NR

1 3 5 7 9 10 8 6 4 2

ISBN 09546309-1-2

Conceived and produced by Elwin Street Limited
www.elwinstreet.com

Designer: Jon Wainwright, Alchemedia
Copyeditor: Toria Leitch

Front cover image: Getty
Back cover images (from left to right): Science Photo Library, Getty,
Environmental Criminology Research Inc., Getty

See page 176 for other picture credits.

Printed in China

"And the murderer?"

"Is a tall man, left-handed, limps with the right leg, wears thick-soled shooting-boots and a gray cloak, smokes Indian cigars, uses a cigar-holder, and carries a blunt pen-knife in his pocket. There are several other indications, but these may be enough to aid us in our research."

Sherlock Holmes, from *The Boscombe Valley Mystery*

CONTENTS

FOREWORD

Annoying though it must be for its practitioners, criminal profiling only began to acquire public awareness with the runaway success of Thomas Harris's *The Silence of the Lambs*. That novel and the subsequent film created a picture in people's minds of the profiler as almost superhuman – he or she could examine a crime scene and instantly see what was invisible to the rest of us. From that, it was an easy step to conjure up the crucial elements of the personality behind it. To the lay person, it seemed a heady mixture of science and witchcraft. To me as a crime writer, it seemed rich with potential for novels that would explore both its possibilities and the inevitable conflicts between this new discipline and more conventional methods of detection.

When I began in 1993 to research *The Mermaids Singing*, which went on to win the Gold Dagger for best crime novel of the year, I struggled to find the information I knew I needed to underpin the creation of Dr. Tony Hill, my psychological profiler. There were clinical psychology textbooks, of course, but these were largely impenetrable to an outsider like me. Some of the early FBI profilers were beginning to write memoirs about their cases, but while these were interesting, they neither lifted the veil on the process nor did they provide any kind of critical analysis of their methodology. The only remotely helpful book I could find was the FBI's Behavioral Sciences Unit's *Sexual Homicide*. And that left me asking more questions than it answered.

My problem was made worse because, unlike the US, where detectives are trained to be profilers, in the UK, we have traditionally used clinical and academic practitioners to work

8

alongside police officers, which does
create a different set of parameters and
their accompanying tensions.

I finally resolved my difficulties
when I tracked down a real live profiler,
clinical psychologist Mike Berry, who
was prepared to share with me the
process he uses to draw up a suspect
profile for the police.

Since those early days, much has
been written about criminal profiling,
either by its practitioners or by
academics. Both groups have their
limitations. Practitioners always have
reputations to protect; academics have
theories to propound and defend.
Practitioners seek to entertain as well as

to inform; academics are prone to slide into obscure jargon that leaves
most of us gasping for air. What was missing was an overview of
criminal profiling that examined the various approaches, critically
reviewed their strengths and weaknesses, and explored the value of their
applications in live cases.

This is precisely what Wayne Petherick has given us in this tome.
He strips away the myths and misconceptions to provide an accessible guide
to one of the most fascinating forensic disciplines used to catch criminals.
From the earliest cases where it was used, he takes us through the processes
used by its practitioners, revealing successes and failures along the way.
He is not afraid to turn a critical light on each different methodology,
exposing its limitations as well as its possibilities. And he does all of this in
direct and straightforward language that illuminates rather than obscures.

But this book is far more than a research tool for writers. It's an
absorbing excursion into an aspect of detection that should fascinate
anyone who is interested in the reasons human beings behave as we do.
Wayne Petherick has opened the door and let the light in. And I for one
am grateful.

Val McDermid

INTRODUCTION

The modern public has a longstanding fascination – even obsession – with sensational crimes and those who commit them. The public wants to know *who*, the public wants to know *why*, and the public wants the lurid details of *how*. Primarily, there are two needs that seem to drive this interest to understand crime and criminals. First, there is a prurient need to revel in the darker sides of human behavior; a need to be shocked or frightened or sickened – but from a safe distance, like warmth from a fire. Second, there is a need to label criminals in such a way that they are separate from *us*; that *they* are not the same as *we*. This to prove that criminals are monstrous deviations from the norm, and what lives in *them* could not possibly live inside any of *us*.

In the past two hundred years, with the evolution of the media, this public appetite has been fed an increasing diet of human carnage.

The 1800s saw the beginning of the age of intense media coverage of crime, arguably, with the Whitechapel murders in England (1888), and then in the United States with the trial of Elizabeth "Lizzie" Borden for the murders of Andrew and Abby Borden, her father and stepmother, in Massachusetts (1893). The public craved specifics and narration, and the media eagerly obliged. Crime was good for business, it could be said.

In the 1900s the international media grew to meet an increasing demand for the coverage and even sensationalization of crime and criminals. Examples include:

1 the trial and execution of Henri Landru, France's infamous "Bluebeard" (1921)
2 the trial and executions of Nicola Sacco and Bartolomeo Vanzetti for the Braintree, Massachusetts payroll robbery and murders (1920s)
3 the trial of Richard Loeb and Nathan Leopold for the kidnap and murder of Bobbie Franks in Chicago, Illinois (1924)
4 the trial and execution of Bruno Richard Hauptmann for the kidnap and murder of Charles Lindbergh Jr. in New Jersey (1930s)
5 the trials of Sam Sheppard for the murder of his wife, Marilyn, in Ohio (1950s–1960s)

6 the trial of Charles Manson and his followers in California (1970s)

7 the trial of New York subway vigilante Bernard Goetz (1987)

8 the California trial of O.J. Simpson for the double murder of his wife, Nicole, and Ron Goldman (1994)

9 the California trial of Lyle and Erik Menendez for the shotgun killings of their parents, Jose and Kitty Menendez (1996)

These to name only an infamous few. The seemingly endless public demand for details of their crimes has undeniably made celebrities of them all. The more dramatic the contrasts in a case, the better.

Enter the criminal profiler. A true criminal profiler is one who examines criminal behavior in order to understand an offender's various characteristics. However, the public has often demanded more from criminal profilers than they are truly able to provide. Ultimately, a criminal profiler myth was born to meet this demand – a myth of perfect insight into the criminal which the public has been eager to consume at every opportunity.

Not since the detective has there been a profession that has so deeply captured the imagination of the public, as well as being so ripe for exaggeration. The media image of the criminal profiler is that of a dark and brooding soul, capable of getting inside the minds of criminals, deeply troubled and jaded by the horrors they have directly witnessed and completely understood. Built on films and embellished memoirs, this contrived media image is several levels up from the truth. But it makes for good drama. Rarely now is there a major violent crime committed for which the opinions of criminal profilers are not sought out by the media. The public cannot seem to get enough. The fascination with criminal profilers and what they know, or claim to know, reached a never-before-seen apex in the Fall of 2002 when a series of related sniper attacks began during the first days of October, in Washington DC. What occurred as a part of the intense, wall-to-wall coverage of the investigation that ensued, which lasted at least four weeks, was a threefold watershed event in the history of criminal profiling.

First, the public was exposed to more criminal profilers, and their divergent methods and opinions, on the same case, at the same time, than ever before. This media saturation by profilers was made all the more unique by the fact that it was available around the clock through almost every major news outlet on the globe.

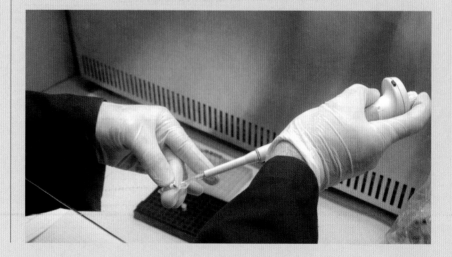

Right A forensic scientist prepares DNA samples for analysis at the Louisiana State Police Crime Lab. DNA evidence processed from this lab led to the identification of Derrick Todd Lee as the suspected serial killer of several women in southern Louisiana in May 2003.

Second, criminal profilers (and the authorities) were commenting and opining about criminal behavior in real time, as events unfolded, and the offenders were responding.

Finally, the global public was exposed to the very real fallibility of criminal profilers and their opinions.

The issue of fallibility brings the criminal profiler back down to earth with the rest of us mortals where they belong. Criminal profiling is a not a mystical art with runes and revelations as many have reported in the news and even suggested in court testimony. It is a skill that can be taught, learned, and within which mistakes can be made.

The public has many sources available when seeking to learn what criminal profiling actually is and what criminal profilers are actually capable of. Primarily there are works of fiction, including books, movies, and TV shows. These are almost entirely inaccurate dramatic portrayals of near psychics. Then there are supposed non-fiction sources, including memoirs, media accounts, and works of true crime. However these are also susceptible to exaggeration and embellishment, as drama increases sales and even the news is in the business of selling itself. The most reliable source of information about criminal profiling exists in the professional literature, in scholarly journal articles and textbooks on the subject. But these are often too wordy and too complex for the general public to digest, and are subsequently ignored by the media aside from the vague reference.

As it stands, then, the majority of public opinion regarding criminal profiling and criminal profilers comes from mass-media and pop-culture sources. From these sources, an accurate understanding is all but impossible. A gap exists, between what is believed of criminal profilers and what they are genuinely capable of, because of the media's race to feed the public's undying demand for violent and sensational crime.

This book is an attempt by its author to bridge that gap between the myth of the criminal profiler that has so often betrayed public confidence, and the real work that is being done by criminal profilers today. The details of crimes are provided and shown to educate rather than titillate, and the human carnage is shown to have human consequence. For those who wish to understand the genuine capabilities of criminal profilers, without hype or hyperbole, this is an excellent place to begin.

Brent E. Turvey, MS

chapter 1

ORIGINS AND HISTORY OF PROFILING

Thanks to media portrayals of the profiler and
the profiling process, recognition of the work of these
forensic detectives has been brought into our homes.
However, not all of these portrayals provide an
accurate picture of the field, and they tend to
represent the profiler as a super sleuth, capable
of solving even the most obscure and mystifying
crimes. The truth is more complicated.

Opposite John Duffy, the "Railway Rapist," was tracked down in 1988 with the help of a psychological profile.

ORIGINS OF PROFILING

Since the early days of criminal investigation, detectives have been tested by cases that were hard to solve using traditional methods of inquiry. Profiling is a relatively recent investigative tool that has meant that some such cases are now solvable.

PROFILING: FACT AND FICTION

The fictional profiler is usually cast as a dark, introspective, and brooding character who possesses a keen and penetrating insight into the criminal mind. Their investigations are aided by flashbacks, affording them a minds-eye view into the crime as it happened and suggesting that they possess powers beyond that of a normal detective. This can have a surprising and functional impact in the field of profiling – by convincing others that they alone possess these qualities, profilers can persuade the public that they are the only one with the abilities required to solve the most complex crimes and catch the most elusive criminals. This allows them to corner the market for themselves, while at the same time denying the skills of a number of independent practitioners who do not seemingly possess the "profiling gene."

Despite the obvious differences between fiction and reality, in what other ways do these tales match up to the reality of the profiler's duties or capabilities? In what ways do they differ? These subjects and others are the focus of this book, which examines, from a critical point of view, the historical development of profiling and the current state of the art. It debunks some of the mythology and lore that has become entrenched in both true-crime and academic representations, and provides an overview of the different methods employed within the profiling community.

THE FIRST DETECTIVES AND NEW TOOLS

Detectives have grappled with hard-to-crack cases for hundreds of years. Such cases may have no witnesses or physical evidence, or the criminal may have manipulated the evidence so as to throw investigators off track. While many of these crimes may eventually be solved, some

Left James Watson (left) and Francis Crick (right), the discoverers of the structure of DNA, with their model of the DNA molecule in 1953. Watson, Crick, and X-ray crystallography researcher Maurice Wilkins shared the 1962 Nobel Prize for Physiology or Medicine.

undoubtedly experience a period of inactivity, while others still, regardless of the passage of time, go unsolved.

In cases that have been solved, investigators may have had to rely on luck, often having to wait until there was a break in the case, or they may even have sought the help of psychics. However, an important development in the world of crime fighting has been the evolution of new technologies. The invention of the first fingerprint system by Francis Galton, the introduction of ballistics and criminalistics into police work by Eugène François Vidocq, and the more recent discovery of the molecular basis of genetics by Watson and Crick, have all meant that more and more crimes can be brought to a successful close. While these tools rely on the interpretation of physical evidence through scientific analysis, within the last century or so a new tool has emerged which goes beyond physical evidence. This new tool is criminal profiling.

THE HISTORY OF PROFILING

Criminal profiling affords police a critical insight into an offender and their crime. It may help to understand why an offender has chosen a particular weapon, why they chose a particular victim, or why they chose a particular geographic region in which to offend. It may answer questions outside the realm of experience of even the most seasoned detective, such as the motivation behind a crime, and it may also help the police in developing a line of questioning once a suspect has been identified.

Sherlock Holmes: The First Profiler?

Fictional characters – in this case literary detectives – who predate modern-day profilers are just as crucial to the discussion as real-life profilers who set things in motion for the current state-of-the-art world of criminalistics. Undoubtedly, Sherlock Holmes is the character with the greatest historical significance. Interestingly, Arthur Conan Doyle did not base Holmes on a real detective, but on Dr. Joseph Bell, who was his mentor while studying medicine at Edinburgh University. Doyle was ever-amazed at the skill with which Bell would seemingly pluck a patient's history out of the most trivial set of facts or observations.

In *The Sign of Four,* Holmes shows off his talents to his sidekick, Dr. Watson, regarding his observations of a watch in Watson's possession:

"Subject to your correction, I should judge that the watch belonged to your elder brother, who inherited it from your father."

"That you gather, no doubt, from the H. W. upon the back?"

"Quite so. The W suggests your own name. The date of the watch is nearly fifty years back, and the initials are as old as the watch: so it was made for the last generation. Jewelry usually descends to the eldest son, and he is most likely to have the same name as the father. Your father has, if I remember right, been dead many years. It has, therefore, been in the hands of your eldest brother."

"Right, so far," said I. "Anything else?"

"He was a man of untidy habits – very untidy and careless. He was left with good prospects, but he threw away his chances, lived for some time in poverty with occasional short intervals of prosperity, and finally, taking to drink, he died. That is all I can gather."

I sprang from my chair and limped impatiently about the room with considerable bitterness in my heart.

"This is unworthy of you, Holmes," I said. "I could not have believed that you would have descended to this. You have made inquiries into the history of my unhappy brother, and you now pretend to deduce this knowledge in some fanciful way. You cannot expect me to believe that you have read all this from his old watch! It is unkind and, to speak plainly, has a touch of charlatanism in it."

"My dear doctor," said he kindly, "pray accept my apologies. Viewing the matter as an abstract problem, I had forgotten how personal and painful a thing it might be to you. I assure you, however, that I never even knew that you had a brother until you handed me the watch."

"Then how in the name of all that is wonderful did you get these facts? They are absolutely correct in every particular."

"Ah, that is good luck. I could only say what was the balance of probability. I did not at all expect to be so accurate."

"But it was not mere guesswork?"

"No, no: I never guess. It is a shocking habit – destructive to the logical faculty. What seems strange to you is only so because you do not follow my train of thought or observe the small facts upon which large inferences may depend. For example, I began by stating that your brother was careless. When you observe the lower part of that watch-case you notice that it is not only dinted in two places but it is cut and marked all over from the habit of keeping other hard objects, such as coins or keys, in the same pocket. Surely it is no great feat to assume that a man who treats a fifty-guinea watch so cavalierly must be a careless man. Neither is it a very far-fetched inference that a man who inherits one article of such value is pretty well provided for in other respects."

I nodded to show that I followed his reasoning.

"It is very customary for pawnbrokers in England, when they take a watch, to scratch the numbers of the ticket with a pin point upon the inside of the case. It is more handy than a label as there is no risk of the number being lost or transposed. There are no less than four such numbers visible to my lens on the inside of this case. Inference – that your brother was often at low water. Secondary inference – that he had occasional bursts of prosperity, or he could not have redeemed the pledge. Finally, I ask you to look at the inner plate, which contains the keyhole. Look at the thousands of scratches all round the hole – marks where the key has slipped. What sober man's key could have scored those grooves? But you will never see a drunkard's watch without them. He winds it at night, and he leaves these traces of his unsteady hand. Where is the mystery in all this?"

"It is as clear as daylight," I answered. "I regret the injustice which I did you. I should have had more faith in your marvelous faculty. May I ask whether you have any professional inquiry on foot at present?"

Above Sherlock Holmes, created by author Arthur Conan Doyle, is the archetypal detective figure and hero of four novels and 56 short stories which were published between 1887 and 1927 and still sell strongly all over the world.

While Arthur Conan Doyle likely never intended that Holmes would become one of the first fictional profilers, his place in history cannot be overstated. The way Holmes reads the meaning of evidence, and the conclusions he draws from it are not that different to what modern profilers do. There has been much talk, however, even in the stories themselves, of how Holmes employs deductions in arriving at his conclusions. While a good deal of his assessments are based on the evidence, many of them are still open to interpretation and are subject to more than one conclusion. As a result, they are often more akin to induction than deduction, and this is covered in depth in chapter 4.

Is this the face of Jack the Ripper?

James Maybrick: Accused of the murders

Jack the Ripper

Turning to a real-life case, Jack the Ripper fascinates profilers and true-crime buffs alike, with many theories circulating about the possible identity of the offender. He terrorized the streets of Whitechapel, London, in 1888, and the gruesome and vicious nature of the attacks, which claimed the lives of five prostitutes, shocked and paralyzed the community. Sadly, the reality is that we will never know who the real Jack the Ripper was beyond several attempts to suggest the most likely suspect.

In this case, the analyst at the time was not a professional criminal profiler but a police surgeon by the name of Thomas Bond. Initially consulted to provide an assessment of the Ripper's surgical skill, Bond believed that:

" The murderer must have been a man of physical strength and great coolness and daring. There is no evidence he had an accomplice. He must in my opinion be a man subject to periodic attacks of homicidal and erotic mania. The character of the mutilations indicates that the man may be in a condition sexually, that may be called Satyriasis. It is of course possible that the homicidal impulse may have developed from a revengeful or brooding condition of mind, or that religious mania may have been the original disease but I do not think either hypothesis is likely. The murderer in external appearance is quite likely to be a quiet inoffensive looking man probably middle aged and neatly and respectably dressed. I think he might be in the habit of wearing a cloak or overcoat or he could hardly have escaped notice in the streets if the blood on his hands or clothes were visible.

Assuming the murderer be such a person as I have just described, he would be solitary and eccentric in his habits, also he is likely to be a man without regular occupation, but with some small income or pension. He is possibly living among respectable persons who have some knowledge of his character and habits and who may have had grounds for suspicion that he is not quite right in his mind at times. Such persons would probably be unwilling to communicate suspicions to the police for fear of trouble or notoriety, whereas if there were prospect of reward it might overcome their scruples. "

With regards to the surgical and anatomical knowledge displayed by the Ripper, Bond noted that "in each case, the mutilation was inflicted by a person who had no scientific nor anatomical knowledge. In my opinion, he does not even possess the technical knowledge of a butcher or horse slaughterer, or any person accustomed to cutting up dead animals."

Given that there was no apprehension or conviction, it is impossible to measure the accuracy of the profile against anyone. However, while

LANGER'S PROFILE OF ADOLF HITLER'S LIKELY FUTURE ACTIONS

1 Hitler may die of natural causes: This was not considered likely. Aside from one minor ailment (a stomach upset) he was in relatively good physical condition. It was further noted that should Hitler die of natural causes, this would dispel the myth that he was the spawn of some supernatural force.

2 Hitler might seek refuge in a neutral country: Given concern over his immortality, this was not considered likely, as running away at a critical point in the war would almost certainly ruin his supernatural standing.

3 Hitler might get killed in battle: If the war was no longer tenable, this might lead Hitler to ride into battle with his troops, which was considered a very real possibility. This outcome was considered to be among the least preferable – going out in a blaze of glory would solidify the German people and make them fight with renewed vigor.

4 Hitler might be assassinated: While this scenario was possible, it was considered to be highly unlikely given his paranoia and high security protection. Again, this outcome was considered undesirable because it would elevate him to the status of martyr.

5 Hitler may go insane: As he possessed characteristics that bordered on schizophrenia, it was considered a possibility that if faced with defeat he may collapse psychologically, though the possibility of this occurring decreased with time.

6 The German military might revolt and seize him: Given his status among the German people, this was thought to be extremely unlikely. Also, his charismatic nature and his ability to rally his own troops argued against this.

7 Hitler may fall into enemy hands: Langer believed this was the most unlikely possibility of all. Given his fear of being vanquished, it was felt that he would do everything in his power to avoid this.

8 Hitler might commit suicide: Considered to be the most likely scenario because of his previous threats of suicide, Langer also noted that if this outcome did occur Hitler would stage a very dramatic affair or have someone else act as executioner. Again, this was not considered a very favorable possibility because of the effect this would have on rousing the German people and military.

the accuracy cannot be measured, the place of the conclusions in the history of profiling is well-established. It would be approximately 60 years before another major event placed profiling back on the center stage, and made another mark on its development.

Hitler's Profile

While Bond worked from scant information and evidence, Walter Langer, a psychiatrist employed by the Office of Strategic Services (OSS) during World War II, was provided with considerably more information on the subject of his profile. The OSS, the predecessor agency to the CIA, asked Langer to provide a realistic appraisal of Adolf Hitler, to include such things as his current state of mind and his likely future actions. They also wanted information on his ambitions and his motivations. Langer's profile was divided into five general sections: how Hitler viewed himself; how the German people viewed him; how his associates viewed him; psychological analysis and reconstruction; and his likely future behavior.

A great teacher, history, has shown how accurate Langer's determination proved to be. On April 30, 1945, Adolf Hitler committed suicide with his long-time love Eva Braun, in a bunker in Berlin, Germany. As accurate as his profile of Hitler was, Langer's concern about his suicide reinforcing the German war effort was unfounded, with the Nazi war machine crumbling soon after, on May 8, 1945.

Right Walter Langer's profile of Adolf Hitler indicated that the most likely end would be that Hitler commit suicide. On April 30, 1945 he and his lover Eva Braun committed suicide in a Berlin bunker. Today, the site of the bunker is a nondescript parking lot. The German government has decided not to erect any kind of building or memorial on the site in order to avoid it becoming a focal point for fascist groups.

The Mad Bomber of New York

Another example is that of the "Mad Bomber of New York". Beginning in 1940, a series of explosions in many public areas of New York brought fear to citizens and frustrated police. Over a period of approximately 16 years, an unknown person, the Mad Bomber, left a series of explosive packages in movie cinemas and telephone boxes, while others were simply left on the street. A note accompanying the first device, left at the Con Edison building (Con Edison was one company that supplied New York with its electricity) on West 74th Street, broadcast "Con Edison crooks, this is for you". Some of the later devices were left with written communications, others without. Some exploded, others failed. Over time the bombs became more powerful and more sophisticated and one thing was for sure: if the bomber wasn't caught soon, more deaths and injuries would follow.

In an odd twist, when the United States joined World War II in the early 1940s, the bomber sent a letter, made out of clipped letters and words, to police headquarters in Manhattan. The letter was signed F.P., in the usual way, and it must surely have been from the bomber (though no one was quite sure at this stage who, or what, F.P. referred to – it was later revealed by the bomber himself that it stood for "Fair-Play"). Additionally, the letter contained another reference to Con Edison, which, together with mention of some undisclosed treachery, was to characterise the theme of many of the bombings.

Later, the failure of the media to identify and publish information about his crimes appeared to frustrate the bomber, and in 1956 he wrote to the *Herald Tribune*:

" While victims get blasted – the yellow press makes no mention of these ghoulish acts. These same ghouls call me a psychopath – any further reference to me as such – or the like – will be dealt with . . . "

For good reason, the police became increasingly concerned about future crimes and the safety of the public. Numerous attempts to identify a suspect from Con Edison's employment records – the likely suspect pool – had not been fruitful, and police felt it was time to try

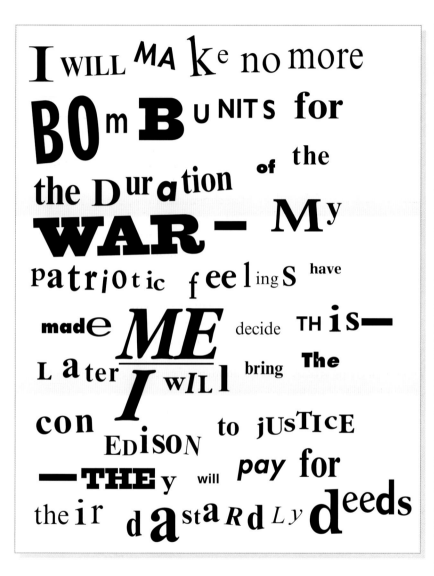

I WILL MAKe no more BOmB UNITs for the Duration of the WAR - My patriotic feelings have made ME decide THis— Later I wILl bring The con EDISON to jUsTIce —THEy will pay for their dastaRdLy deeds

something a little more unconventional, so they consulted Dr. James Brussel, a Greenwich Village psychiatrist. After reviewing the letters and other evidence left by the bomber, Brussel conveyed his profile to police (see page 27).

Above The "Mad Bomber of
New York," George Metesky,
peers out of a jail cell after
his capture in January 1957.

This profile, uncannily accurate in its conclusions but questionable
in its method, has since become part of profiling lore. Perhaps the most
famous of the points is the last, noting what the bomber would be
wearing when arrested. (Even though most of his reasoning is provided
in detail, Brussel doesn't provide much in the way of explanation for
this last point beyond a hunch.) Contrary to popular belief, the
bomber, George Metesky, a foreign-born Roman Catholic who lived
with two older sisters, was actually wearing his pajamas (he was
arrested at night). After officers allowed him to change before escorting
him to the station, he returned from his bedroom – in a navy-blue, pin-
striped, double-breasted suit.

Brussel's full conclusions and the logic behind them are contained in
his memoir *Casebook of a Crime Psychiatrist*. Some of his conclusions
are simply commonsense; others a combination of psychiatric
experience and theory.

BRUSSEL'S PROFILE OF THE MAD BOMBER OF NEW YORK

1   The offender is a male: "I believe this merely because the manufacture of explosives and detonative devices began, and for a long time continued, as a man's job."

2   The bomber is paranoid: The bomber implies several times that Con Edison and others were acting against him. Also, his first device was aimed at Con Edison but his later targets were somewhat more random. This suggested a belief in a conspiracy against him.

3   The bomber was neither thin nor fat: This conclusion was based on the pioneering work of Ernst Kretschmer on body types (see page 28) and the assumption that body type reflects personality.

4   He is middle-aged: When asked how this was derived, Brussel concluded, "Well . . . paranoia develops slowly. It doesn't erupt in its full force before the person is 35. This man has been making and planting his devices for 16 years."

5   The bomber was foreign-born or since his teens had been living with people of foreign extraction: There was a "stilted tone in the letters, a total lack of slang or American colloquialisms." Further, it was believed that the letters had been written in a foreign language and then translated into English.

6   He is unmarried and somewhat of a loner, but likely lives with an older female relative who resembles his mother: This assessment was based on his paranoia, and the way that the letter "W" was written in his letters. Rather than being composed of two Vs, as is usual, Brussel felt that the composition of the W as two Us suggested that the offender had some issues with sex, specifically noting breasts or a scrotum as key issues.

7   The bomber is Slavic: People who used bombs were more likely from Europe, Brussel reasoned, and so were those who used knives (the bomber had used a knife to cut holes in the movie theater seats where he had placed his bombs). When one offender used both, this strengthens the conclusion.

8   If he is Slavic, he will be Roman Catholic: Most Slavs are Catholic.

9   The bomber lives in Connecticut: Some of the packages had been mailed from Westchester County and this was in between Connecticut and New York. Also, there were a large number of Europeans and Eastern Europeans in Connecticut.

10 When you find him, he will be wearing a navy-blue, double-breasted suit, buttoned: Without specifically noting the reasoning behind this decision, Brussel does provide some insight into this conclusion, noting that, "I closed my eyes because I didn't want to see their reaction. I saw the bomber: Impeccably neat, proper. A man who would avoid the newer styles of clothing until long custom had made them conservative. I saw him clearly — much more clearly than the facts really warranted. I knew I was letting my imagination get the better of me."

KRETSCHMER BODY TYPES

Early criminologists attempted to explain the origins of criminality by studying a person's body type. These "somatotype" theorists – from the Greek word *soma*, meaning body – were interested in the link between body type and mental disorder. Ernst Kretschmer identified four body types in the 1950s:

- The **leptosome** or **asthenic** was tall and thin and was likely to be involved in petty theft and fraud.
- The **athletic** had well-developed muscles and was likely to be involved in violent crime.
- The **pyknic** was short and fat and tended to commit crimes involving deception and fraud but may also commit violent crime.
- The **dysplastic** accounted for all other types.

From left to right

Leptosome or asthenic body type, athletic body type, pyknic body type, and dysplastic body type.

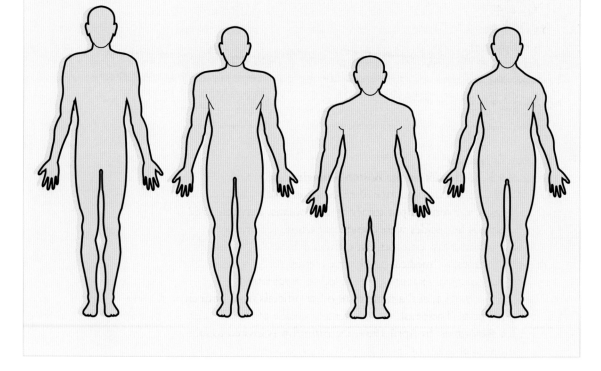

The Boston Strangler

Later, Brussel was to consult on the Boston Strangler case, coming head to head with an assembled committee of experts, purposely gathered to assess the crimes of the serial rapist terrifying Bostonians. Between 1962 and 1964, 13 sexual homicides were committed whose features were similar enough to make law enforcement officers believe they were linked. To examine the crimes, a "medical-psychiatric committee" was assembled and consisted of a medical examiner, psychologist, psychiatrist, anthropologist, sociologist, and a number of other officials from both city and state departments. Their task was to create a profile of the offender responsible for the crimes. In April 1964, Dr. Brussel was invited to join the investigation on account of his successful profile of George Metesky.

Above Albert DeSalvo, convicted of the "Green Man" crimes, confessed also to being the infamous Boston Strangler. In 2002 it was announced that DNA evidence taken from Mary Sullivan, one of the 11 women killed by the Boston Strangler, did not match that of DeSalvo, who police said was the killer.

After John Bottomly, the Assistant Attorney General of Massachusetts, recounted the gruesome details of the Strangler's crimes, the assembled committee was given three weeks to mull over the details, before meeting again on April 29 to provide what advice they could. Arriving at the meeting relatively unsure of his own opinion, Brussel was relieved when the order of speakers placed him last. To his surprise and confusion (despite his own doubt) the entirety of the committee seemed to agree on one main point: Given the age difference between the two groups of victims – one young and one old – and the differences in their sexual behavior, there must be two offenders.

One committee member stated that "because of the difference in MOs, we must assume that more than one man is responsible for these crimes," with another agreeing, though basing his assessment on the different forms of sexual interaction with the victims. In some cases semen was found in the vagina of the victim; in others it was found on the floor, breasts, or in the mouth. This indicated that different types of sex drive were represented – and therefore, most likely, different men.

At the closing of the penultimate member's findings, Brussel found himself blurting out his opinion that all of the crimes were in fact the work of just one offender. His conclusion was based on the fact that all of the victims were female, and that instead of representing a different style of sexual attack, the two different victim types represented the offender's sexual coming of age. (In chapter 4 we will see that an offender's *modus operandi* (MO), those things a criminal does to successfully complete their offense, is not a strong proposition on which to link serial crimes.)

Some seven months later, Albert DeSalvo was arrested for a different crime series, which had become known as the "Green Man" crimes. In prison, he confessed to his psychiatrist that he was also the Boston Strangler, and because he "fit" the profile constructed by Brussel, the police effectively closed the case without filing any charges

Opposite On January 18, 1967, Albert DeSalvo was sentenced to life in prison for the Boston Strangler crimes.

against him. DeSalvo was later killed in prison but it was never proven that he was the Boston Strangler.

In an interesting postscript, a 2002 article published in *The Forensic Examiner* explains how DeSalvo could not be the Boston Strangler because DNA evidence taken from the exhumed body of one of the victims could not be associated with him.

MODERN PROFILING

Just as the early work of Bond, Brussel, and Langer served to shape the entire field of criminal profiling, the work of one police officer served to shape the modern profiling community. Long before the Behavioral Sciences Unit (BSU), immortalized in the movie *The Silence of the Lambs,* came into being, a police officer named Howard Teten began his approach to criminal profiling while with the San Leandro PD in California. Teten was inspired by Dr. Paul Kirk, considered by many to be the father of modern forensic science, and Dr. Brussel of "Mad Bomber" fame, among others. (Brussel was a mentor to Teten until the two had a falling out over methodology – Teten disagreed with the over-reliance on Freudian psychology, something which was falling into disrepute among latter-day behavioral scientists.) Given his academic background in forensic science, medicolegal death investigation, and psychiatry, Teten's approach to profiling probably represents the first multidisciplinary "method" of criminal profiling.

In 1970, as an FBI agent, Teten began teaching his approach to profiling, named Applied Criminology, as part of the FBI National Academy. Later that same year, Teten carried out his first criminal profile in Amarillo, Texas, teaming up with Pat Mullany, who taught the abnormal psychological aspects of profiling. Teten and Mullany took their show on the road, teaching at many other schools around the country, where Teten would discuss how behavior could be inferred from the evidence while Mullany would apply principles of psychology to issues of abnormal behavior.

The new FBI Academy opened in 1972 and their involvement with the Bureau continued with Teten and Mullany stationed there as instructors. In this same year, the Behavioral Sciences Unit was established. Following on the heels of many successful cases they

profiled, word soon spread about this new investigative tool, and many requests came from across the nation seeking help with difficult cases. Given the number of requests pouring in, Special Agents Con Hassel and Tom Strenz were assigned to take over half the teaching of Applied Criminology. Pat Mullany left the FBI in 1975 with Teten going in 1978. Neither he nor Mullany ever headed the BSU.

The next point on the historical continuum is what most people perceive as profiling's beginning. That is, when John Douglas, Robert Ressler, and a number of other now well-known agents came to the BSU. John Douglas joined the Behavioral Sciences Unit in 1977 with Ressler coming some time earlier in the mid 1970s. Their memoirs, *Mindhunter* and *Whoever Fights Monsters* respectively, are among the best-known works in the area of profiling.

The Case of the Railway Rapist

Even though profiling was establishing a foothold in the United States, the craft was relatively unknown in the United Kingdom. That is, until the mid 1980s. Partially as a response to the emergence of profiling in the United States, two Metropolitan Police officers, Detective Chief Superintendent Thelma Wagstaff and Detective Chief Inspector John Grieve, invited psychologist David Canter to Scotland Yard in 1985 to discuss the application of the science of psychology to crime fighting. This was to be put to the test in the investigation of the "Railway Rapist," John Duffy. As Canter noted, he was somewhat unsure of how this may be achieved, but he was intrigued by the prospect (from his own memoir, *Criminal Shadows*) stating:

> ❝ At that time I had never heard of 'profiling,' but the whole idea of reading a criminal's life from the details of how he carries out his crime was enormously appealing. ❞

Opposite John Duffy, the "Railway Rapist." The apprehension of Duffy was a landmark in criminal profiling in the UK. However, although Duffy was first presented as the killer to the police team in the summer of 1986, he was not found guilty until February 1988. Much has been learned from this case, not least that if the material available about Duffy had been used more effectively, he might have been caught earlier.

Railway Rapist Profile v Match to Convicted Offender, John Duffy

Canter's criminal profile of offender	Offender
The killer lives in a small area of northwest London.	Duffy lived in Kilburn, a northwest London suburb.
He is married but does not have children.	Duffy was married, but infertile.
He is a loner, with only one or two male friends.	Duffy had two close male friends only.
He is small in stature.	Duffy was 5 ft 2 in (136 cm) tall.
He has light hair.	Duffy's hair was strawberry blond.
He is in his mid to late twenties.	Duffy was 28 when arrested.
He has a semiskilled job and a good knowledge of the railroad system.	Duffy was a carpenter with British Rail.
He has been arrested by police for aggression.	Duffy had been charged with assaulting his wife.

After the apprehension of John Duffy, it was discovered just how accurate Canter's profile had been. Canter's profile, seen above and compared with the characteristics of the offender himself, had helped identify Duffy as a suspect from a very extensive list. Many of the matches between the profile and Duffy are uncanny.

Since the early days of what came to be known as Investigative Psychology, Canter has continued to advance his approach, conducting a considerable amount of research into many facets of criminal behavior. Among the most prevalent aspects of his profiling method are examinations into offender geographic behavior and what factors may influence this.

Behavioral Evidence Analysis

Up until this point, most approaches to criminal profiling had relied primarily on one of two things: firstly, the information gathered during interviews with incarcerated offenders; and secondly, research studies into common or average offender types and behaviors. Somewhat disillusioned with this emphasis, a forensic scientist, Brent Turvey, developed a profiling method that overcomes many of the problems and pitfalls of other methods.

While an undergraduate student, Turvey had oppotunities to interview convicted offenders in an attempt to gain an understanding of their crimes, in much the same fashion as the agents of the Behavioral Sciences Unit some years before. One of his criminology professors, Gary Perlstein, was on speaking terms with Jerome Brudos, a convicted serial killer, and an interview was arranged. In an attempt to ask educated questions, Turvey spent considerable time examining all of the evidence related to the case before embarking upon his interview in 1991.

At the meeting's end, exhausted after a day of taxing discussion, it dawned on Turvey, who was by now intimately familiar with all aspects of the case, that Brudos had spent a considerable amount of time lying, misleading, and blaming, but never once assuming responsibility. The interview is discussed at some length in the first edition of his bestselling textbook, *Criminal Profiling: An Introduction to Behavioral Evidence Analysis*:

> " I realized how truly naïve my understanding of sex offenders was. I spent five hours with him, and he lied to me almost the entire time. He lied about almost everything he had ever done (or rather, he claimed, everything he hadn't done). The only reason I was not completely taken in by his charming personality and generous, affable nature was the fact that I had reviewed the entire investigative file. "

If offenders lie about what they have done and to whom, how much faith can we have in studies that use this as their entire basis? The answer, Turvey reasoned, was to infer characteristics directly from the offender's behavioral and physical evidence:

> **"** I learned an important lesson through that experience. The lesson was that offenders lie. The only way to get an objective record of the behavior that occurs in a crime scene between a victim and the offender is through the documentation and subsequent reconstruction of forensic evidence. **"**

Taking this experience to heart, Turvey reasoned that a shift in thinking of current approaches to profiling was warranted. He undertook a degree in forensic science at the University of New Haven in Connecticut, and the profiling method born from this realization is known as Behavioral Evidence Analysis. (This method, and all others discussed in this history, are presented at greater length in chapter 3.)

Below Police stand around a chalk outline of a body. While such an outline makes for dramatic television, chalk outlines are only used in exceptional circumstances as, more often than not, they contaminate the crime scene.

From the Past into the Future
Contrary to popular belief, profiling did not exclusively start with the FBI, nor is its modern application solely their domain. Indeed, the history of profiling predates that claimed in many accounts of its evolution.

What is most interesting about a detailed examination of the roots of profiling is what this suggests about the future. What we can see from here on is not only the further development of current methods, but also new methods, more research, and a greater understanding of what each method involves, including those strengths and weaknesses that may support or undermine the utility of a profile in an investigative capacity. It is these issues that we will delve into in the following chapters.

UNREALISTIC EXPECTATIONS OF CRIMINAL PROFILERS

Michael McGrath,
Forensic psychiatrist and criminal profiler with the
Department of Psychiatry & Behavioral Health at
Unity Health System, Rochester, New York

One of the most difficult aspects of criminal profiling is dealing with unrealistic expectations. I do not relish the idea of having to deflate the expectations of those who have received their information about profiling from movies, television, and paperback memoirs, or from the FBI-style boilerplate profiles that list anywhere from 10 to 20 items predicting either behavioral traits or supposed facts about the unknown offender's lifestyle. While such lists may serve initially to impress, the investigative relevance of these lists is often nil. These profiles rely to a great extent on statistically derived inferences, drawn from a flawed study that has never been validated. Using a behavioral evidence analysis approach (see pages 85–92), where one relies on the evidence related to the crime(s) being profiled, one will only be able to offer a limited number of inferences relevant to the investigation, but these few opinions will likely be more reliable. Behavior evidence analysis can be a time-intensive effort.

The astute profiler will need access to all relevant case information and want to be able to take the necessary time to review and distill the data to develop a limited number of supportable inferences from the victimology, crime scene evidence, and forensic testing related to the crime or crime series being profiled. This precludes the quick forming of opinions, but ultimately delivers a more meaningful product.

While criminal profiling remains a viable tool for law enforcement, media glamorization has created a false impression that it is a field not too far from the paranormal, resulting in uncanny descriptions of unknown offenders and that these descriptions often lead to the capture and conviction of these offenders. This is hardly accurate and unfortunately sets a supposed standard that is unrealistic, yet expected, even in law enforcement circles.

chapter 2

MODUS OPERANDI, SIGNATURE, AND MOTIVE

What did the offender do at the crime scene that was necessary to commit the crime? What other clues provide vital insight into their personality and motive? Profilers use a number of conceptual tools that have been specifically designed for the purpose of analyzing these behaviors and their meaning.

Opposite Investigators were baffled by the motive of Ted Bundy's serial killings in the 1970s.

BEHIND THE CRIME

Concepts such as Locard's Exchange Principle, modus operandi, and signature behavior are rooted in forensic science and psychology and offer profilers a means of getting into the mind of the offender.

LOCARD'S EXCHANGE PRINCIPLE

The best place to start in an explanation of a profiler's conceptual toolkit is with Locard's Exchange Principle, one of the most fundamental and important principles in forensic science, criminal investigation, and criminal profiling. Locard's principle revolves around the leaving and taking away of evidence, which is critical, since without evidence we would have nothing to examine. The whole field of profiling relies on the idea that when an offender commits a crime they not only take something of that scene away with them, but also leave something of themselves behind.

The concept was named for Edmond Locard, who was educated in medicine and law. In 1910 he persuaded police in Lyon, France, to give him two rooms and two assistants with which to make a crime lab to test out his theories.

Locard's Exchange Principle has come to mean, in its most simple terms, **every contact leaves a trace**, and while it has been attributed to Locard,

Right French scientist Dr. Edmond Locard established the first rules of the minimum number of minutiae necessary for identification of fingerprints.

EXAMPLE CASE STUDY: LOCARD'S EXCHANGE PRINCIPLE

An offender smashes a window to gain access to a ground-level apartment. As his hand breaks the glass he receives a small cut, leaving a few spots of blood on the broken pane. Reaching inside, he unlocks the door, leaving fingerprints on the handle. As he steps through he picks up some of the glass fragments in the sole of his shoes and cuffs of his pants. He also steps a small amount of dirt from the yard through the house, some of which is taken into his own house from the soles of his shoes.

he didn't specifically coin the term or the function behind it. The closest statement along these lines comes from his classic seven-volume work, *Traité de criminalistique*, published in 1920, in which he writes "it is impossible for a criminal to act, especially considering the intensity of a crime, without leaving traces of his passing." Later, in 1931, regarding the analysis of dust, Locard states "for the microscopic debris that cover our clothes and bodies are the mute witnesses, sure and faithful, of all our movements and of all our encounters."

Consider the example case study above. This example demonstrates the application of the principle: a number of contacts have been made and an equal number of traces of the offender's passing. This includes the blood on the glass, fingerprints on the door handle, glass on his shoes and in his pant cuffs, dirt inside the house, and dirt from the scene that he tracked back into his own house.

Edmond Locard believed that the recognition, documentation, and examination of the nature and extent of physical evidence could be used to associate a criminal with particular locations, items of evidence, and victims. The fact that evidence is transferred from one item or person to another suggests that the two things had previously been in contact.

Though some of Locard's own work focused on dust, the principle carrying his name has been expanded to include all trace evidence such as dust, dirt, blood, paint, oil, and so on. Profiling also makes use of Locard's principle in another variation, that of behavioral and

MO

A criminal's MO derives
from three aims:

1 Success

2 Protect identity

3 Facilitate escape

Factors that contribute
to an offender's MO will
usually include:

1 Location

2 Choice of weapon

3 Victim treatment

4 Disguise and precautions
employed by the criminal

5 How crime scene was
accessed

personality evidence, which Craig Cooley, a forensic scientist with the Death Penalty Trial Assistance Division in Chicago, Illinois, calls **psychological trace evidence**.

MODUS OPERANDI

In general terms, any criminal investigation aims to find answers to six investigative questions. These are who, what, when, where, how, and why. The modus operandi, or MO, involves the *how*, that is, how the offender committed their crime and the steps they took in order to successfully complete that crime.

The Aims of the Offender

A criminal's modus operandi is a functional aspect of their offending, and usually meets any or all of these three aims:

1 To ensure the criminal's success
2 To protect the criminal's identity
3 To facilitate the criminal's escape

Elements that can be classified as MO are virtually inexhaustible and include anything that helps in one or more of the aforementioned three goals.

Nature and Range of MO Behavior

The following list represents the factors that contribute to an offender's MO:

1 Offense location type
2 Use of a weapon in a crime
3 Use of restraints to control a victim
4 Precautionary acts (such as the offender wearing gloves, a mask, a condom, covering the victim's eyes or disguising their voice)
5 Transport to and from the crime scene

There are many factors that can affect an offender's MO, whether related to opportunity or something else. This could involve being interrupted during the offense, or be represented by an opportunity the offender hadn't figured on presenting itself. Additionally, MO can be affected by the passage of time: A criminal can learn that a past action was not successful so should be rethought and changed, or that a particular tactic was effective and can therefore be repeated.

SIGNATURE

The criminal's MO is made up of those actions that were necessary to complete the offense: removing or destroying evidence, altering their appearance, or selecting a well-concealed or infrequently traveled area to commit offenses in. Signature, on the other hand, is a term used to describe anything the offender did that was not necessary for the successful completion of the offense, such as getting a victim to read a script they have prepared, or forcing them to put on specific clothing. Because of this, an offender's signature reflects the emotional or psychological needs of the offender and is suggestive of motive.

Signature is a general term used to describe these unnecessary actions, though in practice signature is made up of two separate but related concepts. The first is **signature behavior** and the second is **signature aspect**. Signature behaviors are the individual crime-related actions. Signature aspect is the overall theme suggested by a group of signature behaviors.

The idea behind signature aspect is that an offender's individual experiences and influences on their upbringing or culture directly impact on their emotional and social development. These influences will come forward in a variety of ways, one of which is crime. The way an offender expresses this individual psychology makes up their signature. If the offender feels the need to emotionally cling to others in real life, this is expressed as attachment in offending. If the offender has problems with temper and rage, these too are expressed behaviorally with the overall theme of anger characterizing their crimes.

Since people who commit offenses are the result of different influences, emotional, and psychological needs, their signature should be fairly distinctive, and may be used by police investigators to tell the difference between offenders who have committed the same type of crime in the same general area.

Signature describes an offender's actions which are unnecessary for the crime

Signature behavior describes individual actions related to an individual crime

Signature aspect describes an overall theme suggested by a group of signature behaviors

One point of confusion is that signature, while currently the best
way to link crimes of the same offender, cannot be used to suggest that
a series of crimes was definitely the work of the one criminal. All we
can say is that strong behavioral evidence exists on which to base such
an assessment. This means that **signature analysis** is not individuating
evidence, despite what some in the field may believe or try to pass it
off as.

Class and Individuating Evidence

One of the many ways we can classify objects or people is by their
membership to certain clearly defined groups, or their individual
characteristics within that group. Membership to a broad group through
shared characteristics is referred to as **class evidence**. This may be sex,
height, hair color, or any other feature that could be categorized. Class
characteristics are usually the result of a controlled process.

Individuation refers to the identification of something specific
within a class on account of its unique characteristics. Individuating
characteristics are usually part of an uncontrolled process, such as the
degree of use and wear of clothing.

As an example, a size 12 tennis shoe would be a class
characteristic, whereas the individual wear patterns, marks, and
scuffs on that shoe would make up the unique and individuating
characteristics.

MODUS OPERANDI OR SIGNATURE?

A rapist grabs a victim and throws them to the ground. There is a minor scuffle and the offender pulls the victim's shirt up over their head. They use a belt to control the victim during the offense, and when they finish the sexual assault (after some time), tell the victim not to move.

What kind of behavior would you classify pulling the shirt up as? Is it MO, done to obscure the offender's identity from the victim, or is it signature, to help the offender think about the victim as someone else?

   The answer to these questions can be found by studying the context in which this single behavior happened, and by asking the right questions about it.

I Had the victim already got a good look at the offender, and would the offender have known this? Would still pulling her shirt up stop her from identifying him? Did the offender say anything like "Don't look at me!"

2 Did the offender do anything that would have required the shirt to be pulled up, such as "foreplay"?

3 Did the offender call the victim a name? Was it their name? Was it another name that was not theirs?

4 Did the offender call out the name to increase the victim's fear? If so, do any other clues suggest this was the reason it was done?

Being able to answer questions such as those above helps provide the context for the offender's behavior and allows the profiler to make a much more informed decision about whether this behavior was related to MO or signature.

Profiling is class evidence, so it tries to identify a class of people, such as those who are known to the victim. It is not individuating evidence, and this means we do not try to pick an individual out of that group of people. If we do, this suggests guilt, which is a radical overstep of the boundaries of profiling.

Context: The Critical Factor

Part of the problem with determining the MO and the signature is that many offender behaviors can be quite ambiguous, with a single behavior possibly meaning several different things. So then, how do we figure out if the behavior under examination is modus operandi or signature?

When interpreting evidence – be it physical, behavioral, or psychological – the profiler needs to know the context in which that evidence came to light, otherwise it will be meaningless. If presented with something that is potentially MO and signature, the easiest and most accurate means of interpretation is therefore to look at the context in which it happened. Consider the example on page 47.

MOTIVE

Motive is concerned with answering the question "why" and can be identified through the offender's signature aspects (the general theme of the crime). Motive can be defined as the need that drives behavior, so the link between signature and motive should be clear.

In order to understand motive and offender behavior, a number of classification systems, called **typologies**, have been developed to help in our understanding of various types of crime. Many of these are offense-specific, such as serial murder typologies, rape typologies, and stalking typologies. Some focus only on certain aspects such as the relationship between the offender and the victim, the behavior of offenders within

---

Opposite Ted Bundy is a striking contrast to the image of the "homicidal maniac." A self-assured, attractive, extroverted graduate who did charity work in his spare time, Bundy had investigators baffled by his motive. Bundy was convicted and executed for three counts of murder but is believed to have been responsible for the murders of up to 50 women between 1974 and 1978.

a certain geography, or the motive, while others focus on a combination of these features – referred to as "multi-axial" typologies.

A useful classification system for motive has recently been provided by Brent Turvey, and his *Behavior Motivation Typology* is based on the earlier work of Nicholas Groth. Then Director of the Connecticut Correctional Institution, Groth, who was a clinical psychologist, studied over 500 rapists to determine the psychology of the offenders. Groth's initial analysis concluded that there are three types of motive at play in rape offenses; power, anger, and sadism.

RELATIONSHIP BETWEEN MODUS OPERANDI, SIGNATURE, AND MOTIVE

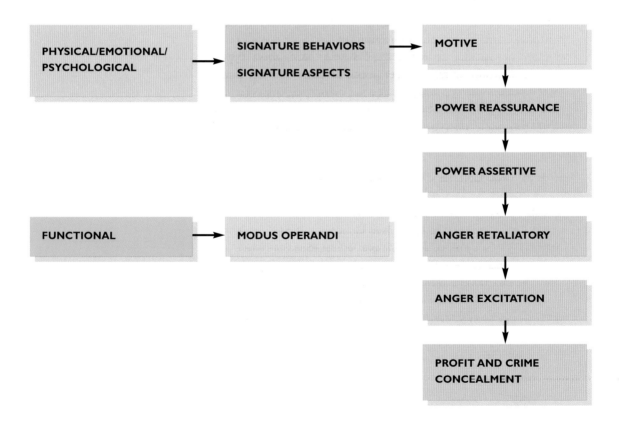

Following on from Groth, in *Practical Aspects of Rape Investigation*, Hazelwood and Burgess adapted his system, adding a further three types:

Types of Motives

1 Power Reassurance
2 Power Assertive
3 Anger Retaliatory
4 Anger Excitation
5 Opportunistic
6 Gang

Turvey later proposed that the last two types Hazelwood and Burgess suggest are actually contexts in which other motives operate and are not discrete motivations in themselves. He therefore excluded opportunistic and gang, and built upon the first four types as main motives. What became known as the **Behavior Motivation Typology** provides a snapshot of an offender at one moment in time. Under a deductive model this typology is used for classifying behavior and not offenders, so should not be used as, or confused with, full criminal profiles. Although this typology originated through the study of rape,

PROFIT AND CRIME CONCEALMENT AS MOTIVES

The motive category of profit is a self-explanatory one and includes any offense in which the offender is driven by the need for money. This may include offenses such as burglary and robbery, and might even include abductions where the purpose is to auction the victim off into sexual or domestic slavery.

In some cases, however, there may also be another motive at play. One example would be when the offender has killed the victim out of rage, and then burns the body in an attempt to destroy the evidence of their original crime. Rage would be their primary motive while crime concealment would be their secondary motive.

Above Ian Brady (left) and Myra Hindley (right) were found guilty of the notorious "Moors Murders." The police recovered the bodies of children from graves on Saddleworth Moor, tape-recordings of screams, and pornographic pictures of bound and naked children which Brady and Hindley had taken. This case has been described as one of the most bestial and perverted in British judicial history and the couple were sentenced to life imprisonment in May 1966.
Opposite Policemen digging at the scene where the body of Moors murder victim Lesley Downey was found.

Turvey believes it can be more broadly applied to other offense types. The power of these classifications is in their ability to determine motive from behavior, and from motive to determine the suspect pool. Each type is not mutually exclusive, since some offenders display more than one motive – although there is usually a primary motive. Let's look at them in more detail now.

Power Reassurance

A reassurance-oriented offense suggests a lack of confidence and feelings of personal inadequacy. Reassurance offenders may also have the distorted belief that the offense is somehow consensual, or that the victim is enjoying what is happening to them (this is how the offender perceives the event and is not a realistic appraisal of the situation).

A small number of these offenders have actually been caught when the victim has figured out their psychology and made another "date." They then report the crime and the next-agreed meeting to police who wait for the arrival of the offender at the arranged location. The needs of such offenders are generally expressed through minimal levels of force, and violence is typically absent – to use force, or to force a non-compliant victim, would shatter the offender's illusion that their behavior was somehow wanted or invited.

It would not be unusual for the offender to compliment the victim, give them advice about locking their doors or windows, ask to see them again, or ask the victim if they are impressed by their sexual prowess.

Power Assertive

Assertive-oriented offenders are actually similar in many ways to their reassurance-oriented counterparts. They too have low self-esteem and a low estimation of their own worth, but their needs are met through more aggressive means, where the offender feels the need to express power, control, and mastery over the victim.

Although the reassurance-oriented offender has some concern for the victim, no matter how distorted this may seem to us on the outside looking in, the assertive offender has no such concern. The victim is merely a tool through which they make themselves feel better.

Assertive behaviors might include verbal commands or threats, profanity, macho, and the ripping and tearing of the victim's clothing. A moderate level of physical force may also be used against the victim.

Anger Retaliatory

Retaliatory offenses could also be titled "revenge offenses," as they are a form of acting-out, owing to some real or imagined wrong. They are suggestive of a great deal of rage or anger toward a specific person, group, or symbol. Retaliatory offenders can be easy to identify since they often voice the reason for their anger, citing how they feel they have been wronged. One stalker from my own case files told his victim, "You think a restraining order can stop me? You are going to pay!"

When violence is involved, offenders may use brutal levels of force or very hostile language, and their crimes may not reflect much planning.

Power assertive crimes are typified by threats, destruction of clothing, and a moderate level of physical force.

Anger retaliatory crimes are the acting out of a perceived wrong. The offender may use brutal levels of force and hostile language.

Anger excitation crimes are those where the offender takes pleasure from inflicting pain and humiliation on his victim.

This is because they offend whenever their anger builds to a point where it creates an anger-related behavior. They often use weapons available at the scene.

Anger Excitation

More often referred to as sadists, these offenders take a great amount of pleasure in the infliction of pain and humiliation on others. In fact, the defining criterion of the sadistic offender is that they gain sexual gratification from the pain or suffering of another person. This suffering can be physical, emotional, or psychological. The behavior of the sadist may include extreme levels of violence, video, or audio recordings of their offense/s, torture, and spending a considerable amount of time with the victim.

LINKAGE BLINDNESS BY LAW ENFORCEMENT

The term "linkage blindness" was introduced by Steven Egger in 1984 to describe the inability of law enforcement to successfully link multiple offenses of the same offender. There are generally three factors that might, either individually or together, create a situation in which linkage blindness occurs:

1 The tendency to place too much emphasis on MO behaviors such as victim, location, and weapon selection.
2 The possibility that more than one predatory offender is operating in or near the same general area as another.
3 Interpersonal or interagency conflicts that can lead to communication breakdowns.

This inability to link offenses may be the result of jurisdictional boundaries, which can be exploited by serial offenders who know that neighboring police jurisdictions do not always share information on

Opposite Henry Lee Lucas confesses to hundreds of murders during his trial in the mid-1980s. Lucas is either one of the worst serial killers in the United States in history, having confessed to thousands of murders, or the victim of a coerced confession. His death penalty was commuted to a life sentence in 1999 due to the controversy surrounding the case.

CRIMINAL DATABASES
Since the 1980s, criminal records, lists of sex offenders, and lists of prison inmates have been collated into computer databases in many countries, crossing most jurisdictions. They have great potential to solve crimes, but concerns about their validity exist.

open cases. The more jurisdictions involved, the worse the situation. For example in the United States there are over 20,000 public law enforcement agencies.

Not only does the term apply to communication barriers that stop the sharing of information, but any other type of barrier which may hinder agencies from identifying a serial offender at work. This might stretch to the deliberate withholding of information due to conflict between offices. When a serial offender is involved, the problem is often exacerbated on account of the social and political pressure placed on law enforcement to solve these serious crimes combined with the desire to be "the one" to catch the criminal responsible.

Another form of communication breakdown that may affect linkage is through the sharing of information about offenses and offense types across borders. In an attempt to address this last issue, some efforts have been made to automate partially the process of case linkage, with many police services turning to computerized database programs. These include ViCAP in the USA and ViCLAS in Canada and Australia. Some regional law enforcement agencies have also developed their own programs such as HITS and CATCHEM.

VICAP AND VICLAS

ViCAP, or the Violent Criminal Apprehension Program, was the brainchild of Pierce Brooks, retired Chief of Police and former Homicide Commander of the Los Angeles Police Department. Brooks grew concerned over time at the sheer volume of information generated during a police inquiry, most notably with serial killers, and devised a computerized solution to the problem. Unfortunately, at the time the idea came about in the 1950s, neither the computers nor communications equipment existed to make the dream of ViCAP a reality, a reality that wouldn't come about until the 1980s.

Several very complex and lengthy homicides (including the Clifford Olsen case) in 1980s Canada forced law enforcement there to rethink the way they organized and prioritized the vast array of information that was generated during these multi-jurisdictional inquiries. The Canadian Police Advisory Committee agreed that a central database to collate and compare information was warranted. Inspector Ron Mackay of the Violent Crimes Analysis Branch of the Royal Canadian

Mounted Police went to study criminal profiling at the FBI Academy and on his return began working on Canada's own "incomplete" computer database, the Major Case Files. Later, Sgt. Greg Johnson was recruited to develop what was to become the Violent Crime Linkage Analysis System, or ViCLAS.

ViCAP and ViCLAS, while complex systems in their own right, basically work in the same way as any searchable database. Information about the crime is recorded in a standardized way (a copy of the ViCAP form can be found at the end of the *Crime Classification Manual*). This data is entered into the computer system as variables, which then become searchable, and the system then provides information on other cases that have the same features. For example, a ViCAP or ViCLAS analyst can search for all rapes where the offender

has broken in through a window using a glasscutter, complimented the lone female occupant during a rape, and tried to contact them again after the assault.

Though their potential to solve complex crimes is high, these computer systems have come under fire in many jurisdictions, with concerns about their validity. In Australia, the state of Victoria has dismantled its ViCLAS program and no longer uses the database. Some police believe that other states will soon follow suit. Also, while the "Mounties" were originally impressed with the ViCAP system, they were worried that the form was too cumbersome for most investigators to complete, although, extraordinarily, the new alternative was even longer.

PRECAUTIONARY ACTS

When an offender sets out to deliberately confuse investigators about their connection to the crime, their connection to the victim, or their identity, these calculated measures are referred to as precautionary acts. The nature and type of such precautionary acts are different depending on the offense and the offender's skill, but there are some fairly common examples, including:

1 Wearing gloves
2 Wearing a ski mask
3 Wearing a condom
4 Altering one's voice
5 Victim selection
6 Disposing of the body in a murder
7 Location or time-of-day selection

HYPOTHETICAL SCENARIOS

1 Precautionary act

After raping and murdering a female victim, the offender places her in her vehicle along with some of his clothing that is spotted with her blood. He siphons off the fuel tank and douses her and the vehicle with fuel, then sets it on fire. His intention is to destroy any evidence which may link him to the victim and the offense.

Above Precautionary act

2 Staging

After raping and murdering a female victim, the offender places the victim in her vehicle and douses it with fuel. Before setting it on fire, he writes a suicide note claiming how things will be better this way, and that she doesn t want anyone to cry over her.

Above Staging

STAGING

The purposeful alteration of the crime and/or the crime scene by the offender. The offender consciously attempts to mask the true motive for the crime by altering the crime scene to suggest false motives.

STAGING

One specific category of precautionary act is known as staging. Any alteration of the physical evidence is referred to as staging, and when an offender "works" the crime scene, they usually do so in an attempt to throw investigators off-track. This destruction or alteration is usually done in order to lead investigators away from the most likely offender; but ironically, it usually has the opposite effect. When an investigator is faced with a staged crime scene, the most logical thing for them to do is to consider who would have most reason to tamper with the evidence.

Vernon Geberth defines a staged crime scene as one in which the evidence has been purposefully altered by the offender to mislead authorities and the investigation. In a 1992 *FBI Law Enforcement Bulletin*, John Douglas and Corinne Munn defined staging as purposefully altering the crime scene prior to the arrival of the police. They also provide two reasons why someone would stage a crime scene. The first is to direct the investigation away from the most logical suspect and the second is to protect the victim or the victim's family. Though the basic definition is agreed upon fairly universally – that staging is the purposeful alteration of the physical evidence – as is their first reason for staging, few agree that protecting the victim or their family is a form of staging. Most sources cite the need for there to be some criminal intent.

Staging is not a new idea, and neither is its recognition a product of recent investigative technologies. One of the first written discussions of staging comes from Hans Gross, in 1924, who refers to the changes made by the offender as "defects of the situation," and that it is:

" just those contradictions, those improbabilities, which occur when one desires to represent the situation as something quite different from that which it really is, and this with the very best intention and the purest belief that one has worked with all of the forethought, craft, and consideration imaginable. "

What Gross is referring to is the careful and deliberate attention given by the offender to the alteration of the evidence. Also, he acknowledges that their perception of how the crime *should* look differs from how a crime of this type *actually* looks. Ultimately, it is this mismatch between perception and reality that may be the offender's undoing.

STAGING AND THE CASE OF THE MARILYN SHEPPARD HOMICIDE

Marilyn Sheppard was murdered on July 4, 1954, in her bedroom. A case was eventually brought against her husband, Dr. Sam Sheppard (whose story inspired the hit film *The Fugitive*). The crime scene showed many elements of staging and there were secondary crime scenes in and around her house.

The evidence suggested that the killer staged this crime scene in order to suggest the following false motives for this crime:

1 a burglary for profit
2 a drug-related burglary
3 a sexually motivated attack

Most of the evidence, however, did not support any of these motives.

1 Burglary for profit – this motive was not long considered a possibility. Police reports indicate that the house did look ransacked but not disturbed to a great extent and there was only a small amount of damage done to the property, something that is at odds with the vicious nature of the attack on Marilyn Shepherd.

2 Drug-related burglary – the only evidence that suggested this was Dr. Shepherd's testimony that there were ampules of morphine missing from his medical bag.

3 Sexually motivated attack – Marilyn Shepherd's body was positioned to suggest that she had been sexually assaulted; however, this motive was discounted on the discovery of blood smears on her ankles along with the blood pattern higher on the bed sheet, both of which suggest that the killer pulled her down toward the foot of the bed and into that position.

In this case the primary focus of the crime was on the victim, not jewelry or sexual attack (see pages 159–163 for more on this case and the role Gregg McCrary's expert evidence played in the trial).

F. Lee Bailey represented Sam Sheppard during his second trial and agreed that the scene was a staged burglary. In a letter to the Chief of the Bay Village Police Department on November 23, 1966, Bailey stated: "The dishevellment of the house appears to be more a cover than a quest for valuables, as the worthless things taken tend to indicate. No burglar would hit a woman 25–35 times. He would run away."

chapter 3

APPROACHES WITHIN CRIMINAL PROFILING

Within criminal profiling there are five individual methods of application commonly in use today. Despite the fact that many profilers give similar definitions of profiling, the way they apply their knowledge can vary. Many approaches adopt a similar basic structure but differ in how the information is collated and presented in the final profile, sometimes leading to significantly different profiles and advice given to investigators. There is much debate within the profiling world about the relative merits of each method.

Opposite Russian serial rapist and killer Andrei Chikatilo was captured with the help of a criminal profile in the 1980s.

FIVE KEY METHODS

The main methods of criminal profiling employ different types of logic or reasoning but share many of the same steps in the development of individual profiles.

DEFINITIONS OF CRIMINAL PROFILING

Firstly, let's be clear about what we mean by "criminal profiling" before taking a look at the five different approaches.

In one of the most often cited definitions, Vernon Geberth, author of *Practical Homicide Investigation*, views profiling as an educated attempt to give investigative agencies specific information about the type of person who committed a certain crime. Geberth touches on the notion that information should be specific, an important facet lost on many who provide profiles so vague they do little to narrow a suspect pool. Brent Turvey states that a criminal profile, in its most basic terms, is the "inference of offender traits from physical or behavioral evidence." He also suggests that criminal profiling is a general term describing any process of inferring personality characteristics of the individual from crime-scene evidence. In Turvey's view, a profile should be a written, court-worthy document accounting for physical and behavioral evidence, since a profile (and the profiler's opinion) could become evidence in a future trial.

The US Federal Bureau of Investigation considers their criminal profiling services to be only one part of the overall process of Criminal Investigative Analysis (CIA). In their view, a criminal profile provides characteristics of unidentified offenders that may differentiate them from the general population. These should be presented in such a way that those who know of or associate with the offender will be able to use the information to identify them.

Criminal Profiling Methods

Following are the five methods of profiling – the first four methods are inductive and the last, deductive:

1 Diagnostic Evaluations (DE)
2 Criminal Investigative Analysis (CIA)
3 Investigative Psychology (IP)
4 Geographic Profiling (Geoprofiling)
5 Behavioral Evidence Analysis (BEA)

DIAGNOSTIC EVALUATIONS

The term "diagnostic evaluation" is a generic term for the profiling services of psychologists and psychiatrists. While not strictly an identifiable method in itself, the considerations of individual psychologists and psychiatrists represent the roots of profiling. Even today, most profiling approaches borrow from psychology and some still refer to "psychological profiling" as a label for the profession.

The application of psychological knowledge is not consistently applied between practitioners, or even among those from the same branch of psychology, so their approach toward criminal profiling is often inconsistent. While you might see some similarity between a CIA, IP, and BEA profile, you may not be as likely to see consistency

PSYCHOLOGICAL AUTOPSY AND THE MYSTERIOUS DEATH OF HOWARD HUGHES

A medical autopsy examines the physical condition of the body in order to determine the cause of death. In cases where the manner of death is unclear, a psychological autopsy – a profile of the psychology of the deceased – may assist in providing evidence for investigators or for legal proceedings.

Consider the case of the Howard Hughes mystery. In 1976 Dr. Raymond Fowler, then President of the American Psychological Association and chair of the Psychology department at the University of Alabama, was commissioned by the coroner to make a psychological study of the world's richest man, who had just died under unusual circumstances and over whose will there was strenuous debate. Fowler used Hughes's diaries and business memos, as well as newspaper articles and interviews to construct a profile of Hughes's psychology, in order to discover how such a vibrant, successful man had become a paranoid recluse.

Some of the points he made include:

1 Hughes was an only child whose mother worried incessantly about germs and that Howard would contract polio. This led her to pull him out of summer camps and socializing.

2 Hughes had avoidant disorder, a means of coping where someone wants friends but is too anxious to make any.

3 Hughes spent more time with horses and in planes learning to fly than with people. His parents died suddenly when he was still a teenager and Hughes suffered depression as a result.

4 At 18, Hughes took over the family oil drilling equipment business and threw himself into becoming the richest magnate of the day.

5 Hughes was in numerous near-death flying accidents in his twenties and thirties.

6 Hughes become a total recluse, spending his days sitting naked on a white chair (presumably in an attempt to avoid germs), watching films.

7 Hughes was terrified of contagious diseases and wouldn't allow employees to speak to him or look at him directly.

8 Hughes became a codeine and Valium addict and moved to Mexico. He wore tissue boxes on his feet, no clothes, and he let his hair and nails grow. Ironically, his teeth rotted from eating candy bars.

In the end Fowler concluded that Howard Hughes was not psychotic. He was able, at any time, to deal rationally with a situation if needed. He clearly had an obsessive-compulsive disorder, yet his fear of germs and desire to live longer than his parents were undermined by his curious behavior after his move to Mexico. The psychological autopsy carried out by Fowler was used as evidence in the legal proceedings after Hughes's death.

between profiles classified as diagnostic evaluations. The end result is usually a product of the individual's understanding of offenders, personality traits, and mental illness.

One example of the approach taken by mental health professionals in the profiling of offenders is provided by Julian Boon, a psychologist in the United Kingdom. Boon examined three cases of extortion and applied different personality theories to each. When undertaking a "diagnostic evaluation," Boon notes that it is important to identify the type of crime under scrutiny (for example, murder), and then move on to specific examinations of it (such as the type of weapon, when and how it was used, and so on). Once this is complete, the psychologist then has the dual task of first selecting which psychological framework is best suited to provide an insight into the crime(s), and secondly identifying which theory or cluster of theories and research will meet the needs of the inquiry. In other words, the characteristics of the case determine the type of theory applied.

In considering whether there is a role for the forensic psychiatrist in criminal profiling, Michael McGrath, a forensic psychiatrist in the state of New York and President of the Academy of Behavioral Profiling, provides a number of suggestions supporting their role:

- The psychiatrist's background places them in a good position to infer personality characteristics from crime scene information.
- The forensic psychiatrist is in a good position to infer the meaning behind signature behaviors (see chapter 2 for more on signature behaviors).
- Given their training, education, and focus on critical and analytical thinking, the forensic psychiatrist is in a good position to "channel their training into a new field."

While these are obviously good areas for mental health specialists to apply their skills, McGrath also warns that the profiler must not fall into the "treatment trap" – the desire to diagnose, evaluate, and prepare to treat the suspect. This, he reminds us, is not the role of the profiler.

Studying the usefulness of diagnostic evaluation is almost impossible since there is no distinct approach and it may therefore be difficult to reproduce the train of thought that a profiler has used to reach their conclusions. Also, the nature of a psychologist's or psychiatrist's training may lead to their assessments being peppered with psychological jargon that might not be of much assistance to investigators looking for direction. Added to this is the fact that many psychologists are not regularly exposed to the needs of a criminal investigation; what they think is required and what is actually required are often two different things. While many of the truly psychological profiles may provide interesting insight into an offender's psychology, their approach may be questionable.

CRIMINAL INVESTIGATIVE ANALYSIS

In modern times, a more scientific and systematic view of criminal psychology has been provided. Putting aside a number of criticisms, the "FBI method" is probably the first profiling approach to move away from individual interpretations of an offender's behavior, and relies on more systematic research.

Development Studies

From 1979 to 1983, agents from the FBI traveled around the United States collecting data for a study that would provide the basis for a profiling approach often referred to as the "organized/disorganized dichotomy." Though this study marks the official beginning of this methodology, both the concepts and the terminology were in use for some time prior to research, with the organized and disorganized terminology evolving in the 1970s as a law enforcement tool. The terms first appeared in *The Lust Murderer* in 1980 as "organized non-social" and "disorganized asocial."

The final report generated after the study, *Sexual Homicide Crime Scenes and Patterns*, would later be published as the book *Sexual Homicides: Patterns and Motives*. Since this time, a number of other works have come about from this study, including the *Crime Classification Manual*, which provides a standard system for investigating and classifying different crimes.

The agents were attempting to draw general patterns of behavior from the data they collected on offenders who participated in the study. The belief is that an understanding of past criminals gives the profiler

Crime Scene Characteristics of the Organized and Disorganized Offender

Psychopathic (Organized) Crime Scene Characteristics	Psychotic (Disorganized) Crime Scene Characteristics
Offense planned	Offense spontaneous
Victim is a targeted stranger	Victim or location known
Personalizes victim	Depersonalizes victim
Controlled conversation	Minimal conversation
Crime scene reflects overall control	Crime scene random and sloppy
Demands submissive victim	Sudden violence to victim
Restraints used	Minimal restraints used
Aggressive acts prior to death	Sexual acts after death
Body hidden	Body left in plain view
Weapon/evidence absent	Evidence/weapon often present
Transports victim	Body left at death scene

Personal Characteristics of the Organized and Disorganized Offender

Psychopathic (Organized) Offender Characteristics	Psychotic (Disorganized) Offender Characteristics
Average to above-average intelligence	Below-average intelligence
Socially competent	Socially inadequate
Skilled work preferred	Unskilled work
Sexually competent	Sexually incompetent
High birth order	Low birth order
Father's work stable	Father's work unstable
Inconsistent childhood discipline	Harsh discipline as a child
Controlled mood during crime	Anxious mood during crime
Use of alcohol with crime	Minimal use of alcohol
Precipitating situational stress	Minimal situational stress
Living with partner	Living alone
Mobility with car in good condition	Lives/works near the crime scene
Follows crime in news media	Minimal interest in the news media
May change jobs or leave town	Significant behavior change

EXAMPLE CASE STUDY: CIA DICHOTOMY

- There is evidence of planning at a crime scene with the offender having brought duct tape, a weapon, and some props.
- The victim has been personalized (treated like a person rather than a prop).
- There have been restraints used on the victim, who has been the subject of aggressive attacks before death.
- The weapon brought to the crime scene has been taken away by the offender, and they have attempted to hide the body.
- This crime scene is organized, and so, therefore, is the offender. As a result, our killer is of average to above-average intelligence, socially competent, had a controlled mood during the crime, and used alcohol. Furthermore, he lives with a partner and was subject to some kind of stressor prior to the crime.

insight into the current offenders who are the subject of ongoing investigations. John Douglas, in his crime memoir *Mindhunter*, puts this same proposition another way: To understand the artist, you must study his work.

Characterizing the Organized and Disorganized Criminal

The concept of Criminal Investigative Analysis is simple, and when using this method the profiler would first assess the level of sophistication of the offense – that is, whether the crime scene is organized or disorganized. Once this has been established, the type of crime scene is matched with its related offender type, listed in the tables on the previous page.

Some time after the original study, the FBI acknowledged that offenders rarely fit neatly into one category or other, and that most will fall somewhere between the two. As Robert Ressler writes in his crime memoir *Whoever Fights Monsters*, "The organized versus disorganized distinction became the great divide, a fundamental way of separating two quite different types of personalities who commit multiple murders. As with most distinctions, this one is almost too simple and too perfect a dichotomy to describe every single case. Some crime scenes, and some murderers, display organized as well as disorganized characteristics, and we call those mixed."

Even though there is a lot of literature on the organized and disorganized approach, there is nothing that details the way in which the "mixed" model would apply to a case. That is, no one has discussed which characteristics are more important than others, or which organized or disorganized offender characteristics apply in certain types of crime, or how they match up with the crime scene characteristics in mixed cases. This point has been the source of a great deal of confusion.

Below Forensic experts investigate the murder of Joseph, Hilda, Tom, and Wendy Cleaver, and the family nurse Margaret Murphy, at Joseph Cleaver's home, Fordingbridge, Britain, in 1986. They were tortured and burnt to death. George Stephenson and John Daly were convicted of the murders and raping Wendy Cleaver in October 1987.

CIA Stage One: Profiling Inputs

In order to start piecing together the profile, all of the information relevant to the crime scene must be assessed, including a description of the crime scene, the weather, and the social and political environment – this is stage one.

Also examined is the victimology: a thorough and comprehensive appraisal of all facets of the victim and their lifestyle, including their domestic setting, employment, reputation, habits, fears, physical condition, personality, criminal history, and any other relevant information. The forensic information such as cause of death, nature of the wounds, and the autopsy report, as well as preliminary police reports, investigative reports, and photographs, are all crucial at this stage. These can reveal the level of risk of the victim, the degree of control exhibited by the offender, the offender's emotional state, and level of criminal sophistication.

CIA Stage Two: Decision Process Models

Here, information from stage one is sorted into meaningful patterns. The homicide type and style refers to whether there are single or multiple victims, and if there is more than one victim, whether it is a *classic* homicide (one person in one location, at one point in time) or *family* homicide. If it is a family mass homicide, with three or more people present and the offender taking his or her own life, it is classified as a *murder-suicide*.

Also included in this stage are examinations of the primary intent of the offender – whether the murder was intentional or the result of some other factors – and an examination of victim and offender risk. In some cases, the offender may have started out committing other offense types (some rapists have started out their criminal careers as burglars), and so escalation is also considered in this stage, as are time and location factors.

Opposite A crime scene photographer captures the exact location of the gun, identified with the yellow evidence marker at a crime scene. The evidence marker helps the investigators remember exactly where at the scene the evidence was found. The photographer wears protective clothing so as not to contaminate the scene as he creates the visual documentation of the evidence.

THE USE OF PROFILING IN CRIMINAL INVESTIGATION

1 PROFILING INPUTS

Crime scene

Physical evidence

Pattern evidence

Body position

Weapons

Victimology

Background

Habits

Family structure

Last seen

Age

Occupation

Forensic Information

Cause of death

Wounds

Pre-/post-mortem sexual acts

Autopsy report

Lab reports

Preliminary Police Report

Background information

Police observation

Time of crime

Who reported crime

Neighborhood socioeconomics

Crime rate

Photos

Aerial

Crime scene

Victim

2 DECISION PROCESS MODELS

Homicide type and style

Primary intent

Victim risk

Offender risk

Escalation

Time of crime

Location factors

FEEDBACK NO. 1

Validation of profile with
    crime/death scene

Evidence

Decision models

Investigation

Recommendations

FEEDBACK NO. 2

New evidence

3 CRIME ASSESSMENT

Reconstruction of the crime

Crime classification

Organized/disorganized

    Victim selection

    Control of victim

    Sequence of crime

Staging

Motivation

Crime scene dynamics

4 CRIMINAL PROFILE

Demographics

Physical characteristics

Habits

Pre-offense behavior leading
    to crime

Post-offense behavior

Recommendations to
    investigation

5 INVESTIGATION

6 APPREHENSION

CIA Stage Three: Crime Assessment

In Crime Assessment, the sequence of events and the behavior of both the victim and the offender is established. Information from the previous stages and a reconstruction of the events which occurred provides the profiler with important elements such as the level of organization or disorganization of the offender, victim selection, control and risk, sequence of the crime, staging, motivation, and crime-scene dynamics.

CIA Stage Four: Criminal Profile

This fourth stage provides the actual criminal profile of the type of person who committed the crime. Once this is generated, a strategy for the investigation can be devised. The profile includes background information such as demographics, physical characteristics, habits,

Left FBI officers train at the Academy located on the United States Marine Corps Base in Quantico, Virginia. The importance of the FBI in US crime investigation came to the fore under J. Edgar Hoover in the mid 1920s against the backdrop of spiralling organized crime. Hoover served as Director of the FBI for a phenomenal 48 years.

beliefs, values, pre- and post-offense behavior. It may also include recommendations for identifying and apprehending the offender and techniques for subsequent interviewing and interrogation.

CIA Stage Five: Investigation and Apprehension

Armed with a profile, investigators figure out if any of the suspects generated fit the bill. If a suspect is identified, apprehended, and confesses to the crimes, the goal of the profile has been achieved. If new evidence comes to the investigating team, the process needs to be re-evaluated and the profile reconsidered. This constitutes stage five, whereas stage six would be the validation of the profile against the person arrested. If a suspect admits guilt, it is important to assess the whole profiling process for its validity.

INVESTIGATIVE PSYCHOLOGY

Investigative Psychology, while still inductive (see chapter 4), uses much larger samples than other statistical approaches, and sticks strictly to principles of experimental psychology, making it much more scientific than Criminal Investigative Analysis.

The evolution of this profiling method happened, it could be said, accidentally. David Canter, then head of Applied Psychology at the University of Surrey, in the UK, was approached by detectives from Scotland Yard who were interested in the application of psychological principles to criminal investigation. Canter's early notoriety came about largely as a result of his profile of John Duffy, dubbed the "Railway Rapist" because his crimes occurred in close proximity to British Rail lines. Little did Canter know at the time, but the principles he applied in the Duffy case were to shape an entire philosophy in the scientific study of crime.

Investigative psychology adopts a five-factor approach to the study of behavior between the victim and the offender. These include: interpersonal coherence; significance of time and place; criminal characteristics; criminal career; and forensic awareness.

IP Factor One: Interpersonal Coherence

Interpersonal coherence refers to the way people adopt a style of behavior when dealing with others, on the assumption that a person's

INVESTIGATIVE PSYCHOLOGY AND THE CASE OF THE RAILWAY RAPIST

From the early to mid 1980s, a series of rapes were committed around London. In some of the attacks, two offenders had been involved, while in others only one. Those offenses committed by one offender usually followed close to those involving two (it wasn't until some time later that a second person was identified as being involved). Links soon became apparent with a series of other, previously unconnected, offenses. The way the crimes happened, the method used to bind the victims, and attempts to conceal the evidence all suggested that despite the geographic distance between them, all these crimes were linked.

Added to the sex crimes, two murders, and later a third, also appeared to share an alarming number of characteristics and the police inquiry was immediately stepped up. Under considerable pressure to find the rapist/murderer, the Police sought the help of psychologist David Canter. John Duffy had previously come to the attention of police, but was suspect number 1,505 on the list. He had been arrested numerous times, once for an assault on his wife and another near an isolated railway station. In the last instance, police felt that despite his being in possession of a knife and some wads of tissue, there was insufficient evidence to charge him. Armed with Canter's profile (listed in brief on page 36), Duffy was moved to number one on the suspect list. He was arrested and charged, being found guilty of four rapes and two murders.

(See pages 34–36 for more information about the Railway Rapist.)

Right Three victims of John Duffy's and/or of his accomplice, David Mulcahy: Alison Day (top), Anne Lock (middle), and Maartje Tamboezer (bottom).

THE SPATIAL MEAN

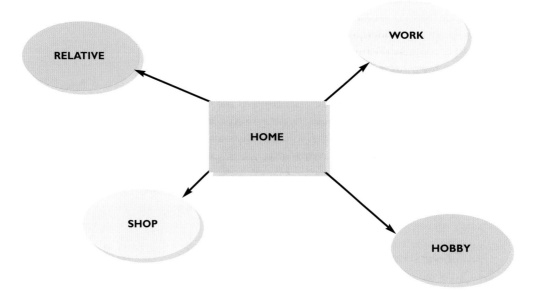

Above David Canter developed a computer program called Dragnet, which aims to predict the likely residential location of an offender from the location of their crime sites. The program considers that the home location can be determined by calculating the spatial mean of the offense locations.

criminal offending is largely a function of their typical, everyday, non-criminal behavior. (This belief is not unique to IP and all profiling approaches rely to some degree on the consistency between "normal" behavior and criminal behavior.) For example, an offender may choose a "model" victim based on a predefined set of criteria they hold: This may include someone who has wronged the offender, someone cherished, or someone else of significant meaning to the offender.

IP Factor Two: The Significance of Time and Place
This argues that both the time and the location of a criminal event may reflect some aspect of the offender's personality or behavior. Criminals often choose when and where to offend, and this may be important in unravelling their psychology. Canter has written a considerable amount on this aspect of Investigative Psychology, known as crime geography.

With crime geography in mind, Canter developed a computer program known as Dragnet, which aims to predict the likely residential location of an offender from the location of their crime sites. The program itself involves a number of highly complex mathematical calculations and weightings, but, as with most geographic-profiling models, operates on some fairly simple assumptions. As a general rule, this considers that the home location – or some other location that the offender is intimately familiar with – can be determined by calculating the **spatial mean** of the offense locations (see the diagram opposite).

One of the first geographic models developed by Canter and his colleagues was the **Marauder** and **Commuter**. Marauders strike out from a central base to which they return after the offense, while others are commuters, traveling into an area to commit their offenses, then returning home. Again, a better understanding of the marauder and commuter can be achieved by representing the types graphically (see the diagram below).

IP Factor Three: Criminal Characteristics

Criminal characteristics help the profiler to understand the type of crime they are dealing with and to distinguish between different types

Below The typical "Marauder" strikes out from a central base to which they return after the offense. The "Commuter," on the other hand, travels to an area to commit their offenses and then returns home.

THE MARAUDER

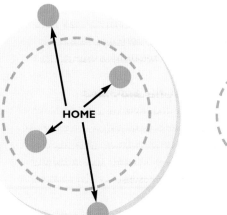

THE COMMUTER

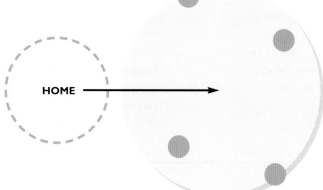

of crimes. In researching this facet, a model has been proposed which identifies the victim as one of three things to the offender: **object, vehicle,** or **person.**

Seeing the victim as little more than an object makes it easier for the offender to carry out criminal acts, for if they cannot view the victim as a person, it becomes easier to hurt or exploit them. For some offenders, this compartmentalization not only helps to make them emotionally neutral during the offense, it also helps them deal with what they have done after the offense; if they do not see the victim as a person, then they will not feel remorse.

In the victim-as-vehicle scenario, the offender literally uses the victim as a vehicle through which they express their wants and desires. The victim is like a prop an actor might use in a play, becoming something through which the offender can fulfill psychological or emotional wants. According to Canter, it is the anger that the offender feels toward himself and the combination of forces beyond their control that are central to offenders who use victims in this way. These offenders cast themselves as the "tragic hero" in a scenario that allows them to express power and control over others that they lack in their everyday life. Offenders of this type may therefore exhibit very assertive behaviors toward their victims – essentially the only people they actually get the chance to dominate or humiliate.

Those who treat their victims with kindness, care and attention, or try to engage them in conversation or the criminal act itself, see their victim as a person. The criminal is very aware and mindful of the victim's individuality and humanity. In fact, this is very important to them. Paradoxically, these men may not even view what they do as wrong. Take for example the rapist who enters an apartment through an open window, telling the victim that they should lock their windows as it simply isn't safe to leave them open.

IP Factor Four: Criminal Career

During any criminal career, offenders behave in relatively consistent ways. However, there is also room for them to adapt and improve on the skills they rely upon to successfully complete their offense. This may be affected by learning during an offense – for instance that breaking glass wakes up neighbors or occupants, or through exposure to the criminal justice system. Offenders also soon discover that leaving fingerprints at a scene is hazardous to their freedom, particularly if they have already been "in the system." Because of this, offenders change and adapt to past situations and circumstances. For example, an offender who now wears gloves or a rapist who now wears condoms may indicate someone who has past experience with the criminal justice system. A rapist who starts to kill his victims may believe, as Duffy did, that getting a good look at him would result in the police getting a detailed description of him, leading to his capture.

IP Factor Five: Forensic Awareness

Along a similar vein, offenders who have spent time in prison, or have had other contact with the criminal justice system, may profit from this forensic awareness, learning what they should or should not do in future crimes to evade capture. This learning, which is essentially an adaptation of their **modus operandi**, is referred to as **forensic**

awareness and suggests certain knowledge the offender may have of police and forensic procedures. For example, the offender who washes away blood and semen, wipes off fingerprints, or hides his identity with clothing is displaying a knowledge that these things can be used for identification. While this knowledge may be acquired by reading true-crime books, or watching television shows such as *CSI*, it is really in the minute details of the changes that their contact with the criminal justice system will be revealed. These things cannot be learned from television or print. Relating to forensic awareness, Canter states:

" Another way in which a criminal's story evolves is by the degree of care he takes in avoiding capture. The person who sees himself as a professional prides himself on not taking what he regards as unacceptable risks . . . The term describes the care that the criminal has taken to ensure that he is not caught. It embraces not just avoidance of leaving fingerprints, but all the other more subtle clues that modern forensic science can make available, such as bodily stains, fibers, facial identity. "

GEOGRAPHIC PROFILING

Following on from the early work of environmental criminologists and the more recent work of investigative psychologists, Kim Rossmo, formerly of the Vancouver Police Department, in Canada, developed his own method of geographic profiling. Rossmo believes that you can get an insight into the locations an offender is most familiar with by examining those areas in which their offenses take place. Information on the crime sites is gathered and then fed into a computer program that analyzes it and applies complex mathematical algorithms to each location, attaches weightings (whether one location is more important than others), and factors in other features of the landscape (such as roads, bridges, and so on). A color-coded map, named a jeopardy surface, is produced from this analysis, which is overlaid onto a

Right These color-coded maps are called "jeopardy surfaces." Information is fed into a computer program which analyzes it and highlights search locations and priorities for the police. This analysis is applied to cases of serial murder, rape, arson, robbery, and bombing.

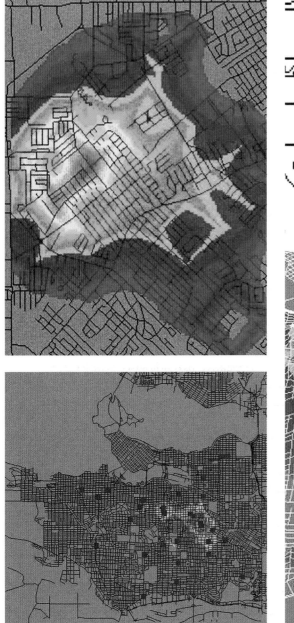

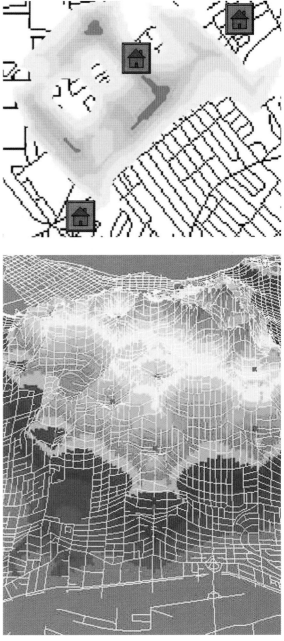

VICTIM SEARCH METHODS

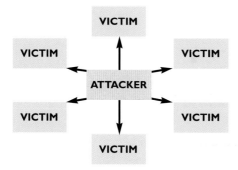

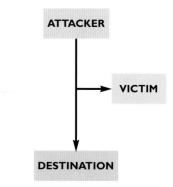

1 Hunter: These offenders strike out from their own residence specifically searching for a victim.

2 Poacher: These offenders typically set out from some activity site other than their residence specifically to find a victim. They may also "commute" to another city in their search.

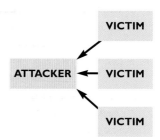

3 Troller: An opportunistic criminal who encounters the victim while engaging in other non-crime related activities.

4 Trapper: These offenders have occupations that may bring them into contact with prospective victims, such as nurses, or those who entice victims into a domain they control, such as their house or work.

normal map of the area: The color-coded areas of the map dictate search locations and priorities for police.

Distance decay, another theory in geographic profiling, suggests a pattern of criminal activity where criminals offend closer to home because the cost to the criminal in terms of time, effort, and money increases the greater distance they travel. This is closely related to the **least effort principle,** which argues that people are essentially lazy and won't do more than is absolutely necessary to carry out actions or behaviors.

ATTACK METHODS

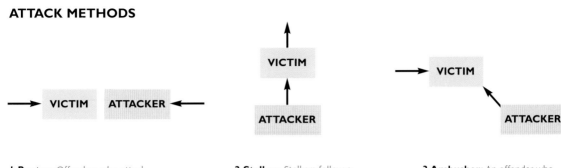

1 Raptor: Offenders who attack a victim on encounter.

2 Stalker: Stalkers follow a victim on encounter and then attack them at some later time.

3 Ambusher: An offender who attacks a victim once they have been lured to a domain in the offender's control.

Some researchers, however, have noted that distance decay and least effort theories do not apply to all crime types, and that some criminals will travel further than others, suggesting that one should be cautious in applying these theories. Consider the Washington Snipers: Profilers placed their residence in several different places, and both offenders lived out of a car.

Approach and Attack Styles

To reflect the predatory nature of violent serial crime, a number of search and attack styles have been developed that may indicate the type of offender or their choice of location. According to Rossmo, in his book *Geographic Profiling*, hunting methods affect the overall distribution of offense sites and it is therefore necessary to use a hunting typology with relevance to particular serial predators.

These **hunting processes** can be broken down into two components: the first being the search for a suitable victim, which influences the victim encounter sites; and the second being the method of attack, which influences the body dump or victim release sites.

BEHAVIORAL EVIDENCE ANALYSIS

Behavioral Evidence Analysis is the most recent addition to the field of criminal profiling and is based on the work of Brent Turvey, a forensic scientist. BEA is a deductive method and the quality of the physical evidence in a case dictates the sophistication of the final profile. No conclusions are drawn about an offender without supporting physical evidence. As with other profiling methods, BEA has stages in which

Above A DNA expert with the FBI points to a rifle used in a gun crime. This gun was key evidence in convicting John Allen Muhammad of the shooting death of Dean Meyers at a gas station in Manassas, Virginia in October 2002.

various types of evidence are collected, examined, and interpreted to develop a profile. Represented graphically opposite, the first three stages are for gathering of information. Recognizing and assessing behavioral patterns is where deduction and the scientific method are applied, in order, finally, to produce convincing offender characteristics.

BEA Stage One: Equivocal Forensic Analysis

In the EFA, all of the available evidence is examined to determine its relevance and meaning to the current case. Since investigations are frequently launched before a profiler has even been consulted, there is usually a mountain of evidence available for that profiler to review. While this information is essentially determined by the nature of the case, most information types are common to all cases.

The EFA is useful for understanding the evidence, helps a profiler to keep objectivity, and suggests the real value of interpretations made by others (such as a pathologist, forensic scientist, or police officer). As noted by Turvey in the second edition of his text:

BEA STAGE ONE: EQUIVOCAL FORENSIC ANALYSIS

All available evidence is examined to determine its meaning and relevance to the case.

"An equivocal forensic analysis is of paramount importance because it helps to preserve the criminal profiler's objectivity by protecting them from investigative assumptions. Many profilers assume that the cases they are asked to review have been thoroughly and competently investigated. They assume that law enforcement and crime lab personnel have worked together to form cohesive, informed theories about victim-offender behavior and basic crime scene characteristics . . . Many profilers do not see the need to question the assumptions of law enforcement or the conclusions of forensic personnel. They view it as bad form, or perhaps even as impolite. Nothing could be further from the truth."

BEHAVIORAL EVIDENCE ANALYSIS

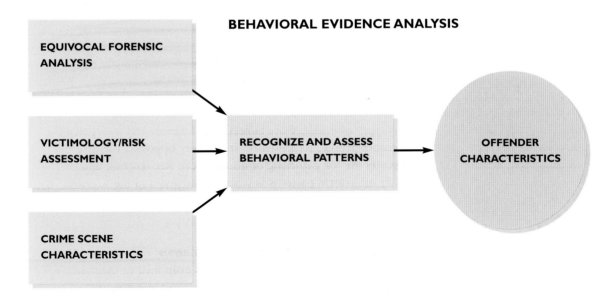

EQUIVOCAL FORENSIC ANALYSIS

VICTIMOLOGY/RISK ASSESSMENT

CRIME SCENE CHARACTERISTICS

RECOGNIZE AND ASSESS BEHAVIORAL PATTERNS

OFFENDER CHARACTERISTICS

BEA STAGE TWO:
VICTIMOLOGY/RISK
ASSESSMENT

Features of the victim's
lifestyle and situation are
examined. This helps the
profiler to understand the
personality of the victim
and perhaps why they
were chosen by a
particular offender. It
allows the profiler to
understand risk.

BEA Stage Two: Victimology

In the next stage, all features of the victim's lifestyle and situation are examined. This, Turvey argues, provides the profiler with the necessary and relevant information to understand the personality of the victim, and perhaps why they were chosen by a particular offender.

Victimology also provides context, connections, and investigative direction, but most importantly, allows the profiler to understand risk. One of the ways that the victim-offender relationship can be assessed is to determine the **type and level of risk** involved – the degree of possibility of suffering harm or loss. Both the risk to the victim and the risk to the offender must be considered.

In general terms, risk can be identified as either low, medium, or high. A low lifestyle-risk victim is someone whose personal, professional, or social life does not usually expose them to the possibility of suffering harm or loss. The same theme would apply for a medium-risk victim, whose personal, professional, or social life does not usually expose them to the possibility of suffering harm or loss, and so on. The lifestyle risk is a relatively stable factor in a person's victimology.

It is possible for someone to be generally low risk throughout their life, and expose themselves to occasional uncharacteristic risks. To account for this, Turvey also distinguishes between someone's **lifestyle risk** and their **incident risk**, which is the risk at the moment an offender acquires a victim, and is related to the victim's state of mind and other hazards in their immediate environment.

Lifestyle risk

There are a number of factors that can increase a victim's lifestyle risk, and some of these may include:

- Aggressiveness
- Anger
- Impulsivity
- Passivity
- Low self-esteem
- History of self-harm

EXAMPLE CASE STUDY: MISTAKEN IDENTITY

A 21-year-old university student attends a theme party where everyone is to come dressed as something starting with "D." He decides (for a "good laugh") to go dressed as a drag queen, in fishnet stockings and thick makeup.

After the party, he calls a taxi, but is told that it is a busy night and it will be several hours before one is available. He sets off on the approximately 45-minute walk home. About halfway home, still in drag, he is accosted by a male who severely beats him all the while shouting, "All queers get what is coming to them," and "Thanks for AIDS, fag."

The offender is also subject to risk. **Modus operandi (MO) risk** is the level of precaution, skill, and planning of the offender in order to successfully complete their crime. The more precautions, skill, and planning an offender uses, the lower their MO risk. So an offender who wears gloves, disguises identifiable physical features such as tattoos, wears a condom, and cleans up after a rape would be at a considerably lower MO risk than an offender who does none of these things, or one who may give the victim things that may directly identify them. (There are examples of offenders who have given victims their phone numbers – not a good plan to escape identification.)

An offender's incident risk refers to the amount of exposure to harm or loss that we, as profilers, assign to an offender. The goal is to understand the offender's perspective and how this may influence their decision to offend.

Incident risk
Some of the factors that can affect a victim's incident risk include:

- Victim lifestyle risk
- State of mind

This stage gathers the general distinguishing features of a crime scene, suggested by the offender's decisions regarding victim and location. It also includes the offender's method of approach and method of attack.

All the information from stages 1–3 are compiled and assessed. Only four things can be deduced:

1 Evidence of criminal skill
2 Knowledge of victim
3 Knowledge of crime scene
4 Knowledge of method and materials

- Time of occurrence
- Location of occurrence
- Number of victims
- Drug and alcohol use

Consider the example on page 89. Here the offender believes they are assaulting a homosexual drag queen, who they consider will not receive a sympathetic ear from law enforcement, if they even report the crime at all. Unbeknown to the assaulter, they have not beaten up a drag queen but a 21-year-old heterosexual who will probably report the crime and will, in all likelihood, be taken very seriously by police. If the offender knew the correct circumstances rather than just making an assumption based on what they see, they probably would not have offended in this way, with this particular victim.

BEA Stage Three: Crime Scene Characteristics

The last stage in BEA, before the profile is generated, is gathering crime scene characteristics – the general distinguishing features of a crime scene as suggested by an offender's decisions regarding the victim and the location. These places may have some meaning to the offender, or they may simply be functional because of their remoteness, darkness, or accessibility.

Another major component is the way the offender approached the victim, referred to as the **method of approach**, and the way the offender overpowered the victim's defenses, referred to as the **method of attack**. In the past, these have been identified as having surprise, con, and blitz components, but as Turvey points out, blitz is not actually an approach, but an attack. Also, the terms "surprise" and "con" are not suited to a method of attack, which implies force.

BEA Stage Four: Profile Characteristics

Finally, all of the information from the previous stages is compiled, and any behavioral patterns are assessed and recognized. Turvey argues that the best way to approach a profile characteristic is to define that characteristic, such as "criminal skill," and then describe the physical and behavioral evidence which supports that conclusion. This allows us to provide a profile using deductive logic.

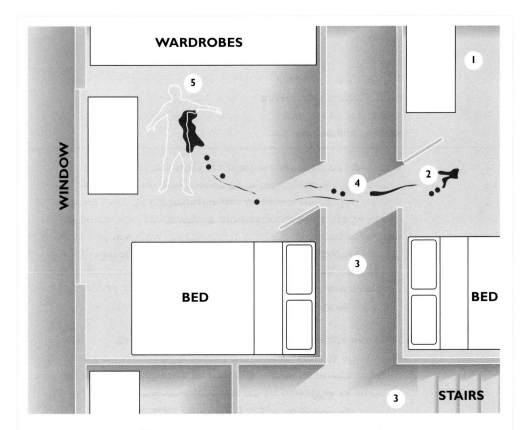

FIVE TYPES OF CRIME SCENE IDENTIFIED BY TURVEY

1 Point of Contact: The precise location where the offender and the victim came into contact.

2 Primary Crime Scene: Where the majority of the offender-victim interaction took place. It is usually the location where most of the time was spent, and where most of the physical evidence was left during the offense.

3 Secondary Crime Scene: The location where some of the victim-offender interaction took place, but not all of it. There can be several secondary scenes associated with one criminal event.

4 Intermediate Scene: A form of secondary crime scene in any location between the primary crime scene and the dump site. Essentially, all crime scenes are primary or secondary scenes.

5 Dump/Disposal Site:: The place where the victim's body comes to rest. This usually only applies in crimes such as murder.

Whereas other criminal profiling methods cast a broad net in terms of the profile characteristics given, Turvey argues that there are only four things you can establish deductively, all of which are relevant to investigators.

1 **Evidence of Criminal Skill:** Offenders who commit certain types of crime often become more adept in its commission. The skill they show may be a function of their planning and precautionary acts.

2 **Knowledge of the Victim:** The choices an offender makes may give us insight into the knowledge they have of the victim. This may come from the use of the victim's name during the crime, the absence of forced entry into their residence, and evidence of more force than is necessary to kill the victim.

3 **Knowledge of the Crime Scene:** Offenders who display a specific and particular knowledge of a location may be familiar with it, and this can provide insight into their geographic behavior. Familiarity with a location may be displayed by security schedules, the location of valuables such as safes, and knowledge about objects used to carry out the offense, available at the scene.

4 **Knowledge of Methods and Materials:** Some criminals exhibit behavior that suggests they possess knowledge not held by the average person. This might include driving a manual vehicle or flying a helicopter, and these things may be elicited through a detailed examination of the MO and signature behaviors.

A BEA APPROACH TO TWO CASE STUDIES

Louis Peoples Serial Homicide

On September 16, 1997, an unknown offender went onto the grounds of Cal-Spray Dry Company, vandalizing vehicles and shooting at employees. Thomas Harrison, shot in the stomach and thigh, described the offender as a white adult male, 5 feet 9 inches, about 160 pounds in weight. He was wearing dark clothes and a cap.

Five weeks later, the Stockton, California, branch of the Bank of the West was held up at gunpoint. A white male entered the bank wearing a black hat, black jacket, and dark glasses. He approached a teller, handing him a note which read: "Give me all of your 100s,

50s, 20s, 10s, and nobody will get shot." He produced a small handgun as the teller got the notes, and then he fled the bank.

Five days later, a telephone call was made to Charter Way Tow of Stockton. Tow driver James Loper attended the scene. No reports of trouble were mentioned during the 3.30 a.m. radio call to the dispatcher. Loper was found by Sheriff's Deputies at 3.48 a.m. He had been shot 10 times.

The body of Stephen Chacko was found on November 4, 1997, in front of Mayfair Discount Liquors and Tobacco. Mr. Chacko had been shot five times. It was found that during the robbery the offender fired at the cash register in an attempt to open it, but these attempts failed.

About a week later, Besun Yu and Jun Gao were shot and killed during a robbery at the Village Oaks Market, again in Stockton. The offender came in through the front door, shot Besen Yu at the cash register, and then shot Jun Gao in the aisle. The offender took the cash register out of the checkout stand and left the store.

Investigators linked the cases through ballistics evidence and called in criminal profiler Brent Turvey. The collection of facts suggested to Turvey that the offender was becoming more desperate in his attempts. He had tried to shoot a cash register open unsuccessfully, had stolen another cash register, which he also couldn't open, and had shot staff who might have helped him open the cash registers.

The offender took precautions in all of the crimes, wearing a hat, sunglasses, and a jacket. In some cases he had a good knowledge of the layout of the premises and had an escape plan.

Oddly enough, despite his preparation, the offender did a number of things that seemed to contradict the purpose of his precautionary acts and increase his chances of apprehension. During the Cal-Spray attack, he spent considerable time at the scene. He repeatedly used a loud firearm and then, during the bank robbery, he waited in line to be seen by a teller. Finally, in an absurd, darkly comical act, shortly after shooting James Loper, he rang Charter Way Tow looking for work, claiming he had heard they were "short a man."

Looking back at the series of crimes, Turvey believed that the Cal-Spray attack provided the greatest insight into the crimes. Turvey suggested that the amount of time spent at Cal-Spray, the damage to cars, familiarity with the location, and entrance and exit routes all meant they should look for a former employee. When approached with this information, managers of the company informed police that they should seek out a former employee: Louis Peoples.

Peoples was a methamphetamine addict (which affected his behavior during the offenses). When arrested, he led police to the .40-caliber handgun used in the crimes and which he had buried.

West Memphis Three Triple Homicide

In 1993 the bodies of eight-year-olds James Moore, Steve Branch, and Chris Byers were found in a drainage ditch behind the Blue Beacon Truck Stop in Robin Hood Hills of West Memphis, Arkansas.

James Moore had been repeatedly struck about the head and was "hog-tied" with shoelaces. The lack of abrasions around the area where the ligatures were suggested that he was not struggling while these were on. James's cause of death was identified as drowning.

Steve Branch suffered from violent facial and head injuries, and other superficial wounds. Turvey suggested that some of the wound patterns on the body were bite marks – missed during the initial autopsy. Steve Branch was also tied up with shoelaces, but had deep furrows and patterned abrasions on both wrists and ankles, suggesting he was moving while they were on. He also was drowned.

Chris Byers, in addition to multiple head injuries, cuts and stab wounds, had been mutilated – his genetalia had been removed. There were abrasions and furrows around the shoelaces used to bind Byers, suggesting he was also struggling while the ligatures were in place.

Turvey determined that all three victims presented a high risk to the offender. They were traveling in a group and not alone, and children are carefully attended to and missed within a short period of time. However, it was also considered that Chris Byers had a very high-risk lifestyle for the following reasons:

- He was a very defiant child with tendencies toward violent and destructive, anti-social behavior.
- He was susceptible to the attention and approval of others.
- He displayed clear indicators of previous physical and possibly sexual abuse.

Despite the belief of many involved in the case, Turvey concluded that the scene where the boys were found was not the primary crime scene but a secondary one. This was based on the following facts:

- The nature and extent of the stab wounds would have required time, light, and uninterrupted privacy. Search parties were traveling in and out of these woods and it was dark, so the crime must have occurred somewhere else outside of this area.
- The nature and extent of the wounds would have resulted in a huge amount of blood loss, but very little blood was found on the banks of the drainage ditch.
- The injuries inflicted on live victims would have resulted in loud screaming and searchers heard nothing of the kind.

The method of approach was suggestive of someone known to the victims who could quickly gain their trust, something that would have made moving them to a different location easier to accomplish. Turvey argued that the motive was retaliatory, with the victims being punished for real or imagined wrongs, and that James Moore was a collateral victim dying because of his association with Steve Branch and Chris Byers. The anger was directed primarily at Branch and Byers, and it is this that shows the offender's association to those two victims.

Because of the type and number of precautionary acts, it was concluded that the offender had some experience with the criminal justice system. Turvey concluded also that there was only one offender responsible for this crime.

However, a short while after the discovery of the victims, three local youths, Jessie Miskelly, Jason Baldwin, and Damien Echols, were arrested and convicted for the homicides. Investigators had found a "666" printed on a bridge nearby and thought this might be linked to the homicide. The three suspects wore black and listened to heavy metal music. They seemed to be perfect suspects, despite a questionable confession by Miskelly, who is mentally handicapped.

Despite a total lack of physical evidence and no apparent motive, the three youths were convicted. Baldwin received life without parole, Miskelly life plus 40, and Echols sits on death row. Echols's appeals have been unsuccessful to this day.

chapter 4

LOGIC AND REASONING IN CRIMINAL PROFILING

All profilers employ at least one of two forms of logic:
induction and deduction. Whether this comes from intuition,
research, or physical evidence, profiling an offender relies on
some form of logic or reasoning to arrive at a conclusion.
Nevertheless, the correct application of induction and deduction
to a case remains one of the most poorly understood areas of
criminal profiling. The following chapter sets out to redress this
imbalance and provide a more detailed and comprehensive
explanation of each type of logic – one of the most important
tools of the profiler's trade.

Opposite Inductive reasoning was used in the profile of the Baton Rouge serial killer, later identified as Derrick Lee Todd.

METHOD OF REASONING

What is the rational basis on which a profiler makes his or her claim? And how did he or she arrive at such conclusions? The individual experience or intuition of a profiler is not an adequate substitute for a study of evidence leading to a deductive conclusion.

INDUCTION AND DEDUCTION

For reasons unknown, the terms induction and deduction and their application have taken on rather loose meanings. For example, it would not be uncommon to hear someone referring to a "deduction" they have made, which formed the basis of their conclusion, and which was in fact based on past experience – a form of "induction." Even Dr. James Brussel, in his profile of Metesky (see chapter 1), boldly claimed during his meetings with police that many of his profile characteristics were deductions – when they were little more than theories based on contemporary psychiatric knowledge.

There should be some rational basis on which the profiler makes his or her claim. This may be an argument about the common or average offender in cases with similar features (which could make the profile characteristic inductive), or it may be based on some form of physical evidence, such as the offender being able to pick a lock (which would make it a deductive characteristic). Even a profiler who makes an outlandish suggestion may do so from an inductive point of view – that is, based on what they feel or have experienced in any given number of crimes they have investigated in the past. Although this may seem to be a suitable foundation on which to offer a profile, the individual experience of the profiler is no replacement for a detailed and systematic study of available evidence, leading to a deductive conclusion.

Inductive profiling refers to the application of statistical data with the aim of developing an understanding of the offender through reference to similar offenders from the past.

Deductive profiling involves the application of logic and reasoning where conclusions come about directly from the collection and interpretation of evidence in a given case.

Inductive profiling involves the application of statistical data to draw a reasonable conclusion based on likelihoods.

Deductive profiling uses logic to draw conclusions from the collection and interpretation of evidence.

Both forms of logic have two components: **premises** and **conclusions**. In its most simple form, a premise is a piece of evidence or information. For example, a premise based on physical evidence would be that an offender picked a lock. In the absence of any concrete information about the skill of this particular criminal we may draw upon past studies of offenders which suggest that people who commit certain types of crime also have experience with other criminal activities, such as breaking and entering (this would make the conclusions inductive). These studies form our core understanding of such offenders, though it would not apply in all cases. Another logical conclusion we may draw is that the offender has experience picking locks and therefore some level of criminal skill that has been honed through other offense-related operations. This conclusion is based on the physical evidence and a logical interpretation of it, so it is deductive. So then, our conclusion – that the offender has criminal skill – is a direct outgrowth of the original premise that they picked a lock. These two approaches highlight the basic difference between a deductive and an inductive profile.

The following general discussion of both induction and deduction offers a foundational explanation of these methods of reasoning.

INDUCTIVE PROFILING

As we have already seen, an inductive argument is one that is statistical, where an offender's profile is suggested by their similarity to past offenders, or where the profiler argues for certain characteristics based on their own experience. Because of the nature of inductive profiles, they revolve heavily around probabilities, that is, the offender is *probably* like this or that, or the offender is *likely* of a certain disposition or appearance. So then, in an inductive argument, the conclusion is *likely* to be true *if* the premise is true. Regardless of the strength of the probability, some inductive arguments remain a problem. For example:

- **Premise One:** The victims of this serial killer are white.
- **Premise Two:** Most known serial killers kill within their own ethnic group.
- **Premise Three:** Most known serial killers are male.
- **Conclusion:** Our offender is likely to be a white male.

The nature of the above argument is such that each component of the conclusion is more probably true if the premises on which it is based are true. So the proposition that the offender is white, a male, and a serial killer relies on a number of assumptions that may or may not have been established in a given case. The first assumption is that the research on which this generalization is based is valid and reliable.

The second, that the offender in this case is in fact a serial killer – in other words, all cases have been linked to the same offender. If either consideration is not true, then the assumptions on which the profile is based are potentially flawed and incorrect.

Statistical Validity and Reliability

In statistics, it is important to ensure that the tools you are using are **valid** – that is, that they actually measure what they claim to measure. It is equally important that those tools are **reliable**, which means that if the same test or tool was given to a different group or applied in a

Above Police surgeon Thomas Bond's psychological profile of Jack the Ripper made use of inductive reasoning. This illustration, published in a newspaper in 1888, shows police discovering the body of one of Jack the Ripper's victims, probably Catherine Eddowes.

different circumstance, then the results you get would be the same. Essentially, what we are concerned with is whether the effect we are seeing is the result of its actual cause, or whether the effect is the result of some other interference not actually related to the event under study.

What is often forgotten by overzealous profilers is that because inductive profiles are based on probabilities, there is an inbuilt margin of error. Taking the previous example: If we were to give a very generous probability of 75 percent to Premise One and Premise Three, then the probability of both conditions being true is typically around 56 percent. (This result depends on the two conditions applying independently of one another, which is a reasonable assumption in this case. The joint probability is found by simply multiplying the two individual probabilities.) Therefore, the chance that our offender is *both* white and male, based on inductive reasoning, is barely more probable than the outcome of tossing a coin, despite the fact that each independent probability is true approximately three-quarters of the time.

While this hypothetical figure suggests that three-quarters of the time these characteristics will be true, it must also be remembered that a figure of 75 percent suggests an error rate of 25 percent. Unfortunately, some probabilities used by profilers in constructing arguments are not as strong as this. To make matters worse, a whole series of statistical arguments linked together may, depending on the degree of dependence on one another, make it less likely all are true and not more likely.

The Logic of Scientific Discovery
One of the most important works on logic, Karl Popper's *The Logic of Scientific Discovery*, warns against generalized thinking, and cautions:

“It is far from obvious, from a logical point of view, that we are justified in inferring universal statements from singular ones, no matter how numerous; for any conclusion drawn in this way may always turn out to be false: no matter how many instances of white swans we may have observed, this does not justify the conclusion that all swans are white. ”

Inductive Generalization Argument

There are two basic forms of inductive argument, both of which are common in the profiling community. The first, and perhaps most dangerous, is the inductive generalization. What usually happens is that based on a limited number of observations (singular statements), a profiler comes to develop theories about a whole system of behavior (universal statements). An illustration of this is the profiler who sees five cases in which the offender disguises their voice because the victim is known to them. The profiler then claims in later cases that since an offender tried to disguise their voice, this means they know their victim. In other words, they see a few consistent examples of one behavior and believe it is common to all similar instances.

We simply cannot logically argue, even if our experience tells us something applies 100 percent of the time, that it is true of the world and will be in every case we see in the future. Perhaps the best way to think of, and characterize, inductions in profiling are as theories suggested by the evidence that are waiting to be tested against it, and not as conclusions in their own right.

Inductive Statistical Argument

The second type of inductive argument is a statistical argument, which constructs knowledge from studies and research. The truthfulness of these statements is also a matter of statistical probability, and while they generally tend to sound good, they are often fraught with problems and dangers.

Profiles of this nature can be identified by the use of the appropriate qualifiers, which often reflect the level of certainty or confidence that the profiler has in their assessment.

Common Qualifiers
- My experience indicates that . . .
- I have often found that . . .
- It is likely that . . .
- The offender may . . .
- The offender might . . .
- It would be probable that . . .

To complicate matters further, demonstrated in the following examples, it is also possible to pass off an inductive characteristic, even a whole profile, as though it were deductive. There is no doubt that this creates confusion among those seeking to learn more about profiling, but more concerning still is the fact that many profilers themselves don't know they are confusing the two types of profiling. An inductive opinion should have the necessary qualifiers, such as "the offender is *probably* male," which gives insight into the certainty of the conclusion. When this same characteristic is presented as "the offender is male" and the conclusion is drawn without the appropriate physical evidence, then it is an inductive conclusion presented as though it were deductive.

To provide further clarification on induction, following are some examples of profile characteristics that highlight the process of reasoning. These are drawn from actual profiles, freely available in the public domain (though there is not room here to reproduce the profiles in their entirety). The first is from the recent investigation of serial killings in Baton Rouge, which led to the arrest of Derrick Lee Todd. The second is from *An Hour to Kill* by Dale Hudson and Billy Hills. This last profile, as with many inductive profiles, offers insight into the reasoning by stating something along the lines of "this profile is probable."

The Profiler's Opening Caveat

Some profilers are very forthcoming in pointing out the logic they use, whether it be inductive or deductive, while others point it out in some instances and not in others. They may present law enforcement officers with their profile noting its reliance on the "average offender" but conspicuously leave this caveat out of a document tendered for the court, typically because courts aren't terribly receptive to educated guesses. This highlights a recognition among some profilers that their work could be based on the wrong assumptions. Some believe that a profile should always be a written document with the appropriate caveats applied consistently, and that the profile should always be a court-worthy document.

Baton Rouge Serial Homicides

Later identified as Derrick Lee Todd, the Baton Rouge serial killer murdered five women in the Baton Rouge and Lafayette areas of

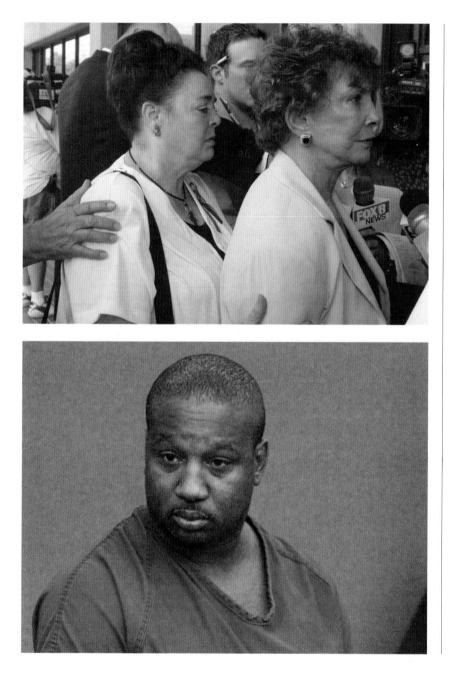

Left The mothers of two victims of the Baton Rouge serial killer Derrick Lee Todd, Ann Pace and Lynne Marino, following Lee Todd's appearance in court in July 2003.

Left Derrick Lee Todd appears in Fulton County Superior Court for an extradition hearing in May 2003. At this time, Lee was wanted for the murders of at least five Louisiana women. He was extradited to Louisiana where he faced charges for the murder of five women in the Baton Rouge and Lafayette areas, including Charlotte Murray Pace and Pam Kinamore.

INDUCTIVE REASONING: BATON ROUGE PROFILE CHARACTERISTICS

1 Based on the age range of the victims and their physical appearances, the age of this male offender is estimated to be somewhere between 25 and 35 years of age.

2 It is likely this offender spends a significant amount of time watching women and following those in whom he is interested. Whether he is at work, at a bar, on his days off, alone or with others, he watches women. At times this behavior could be excessive and something he engages in to the exclusion of other daily activities. Watching women and following them would be

exciting for him. When questioned about it, he would defend this behavior and try to normalize it by telling others "I just like women."

3 His socioeconomic situation is likely average or below average for the Baton Rouge area.

4 These homicides occurred on two Fridays and a Sunday. It is possible that on these days this offender was not accountable to anyone.

Louisiana, in the United States, with most of his crimes occurring around Louisiana State University. He was later linked to the crimes through DNA, and while he is suspected of other crimes, the DNA evidence was not enough to tie him to them. His methods varied with each case, though similarities included the removal of phones from the victim's belongings and a lack of forced entry into their premises.

One victim, Pam Kinamore, was found by a state survey crew near the Whiskey Bay Bridge. They noticed a figure lying in the marshy area below the bridge, and as they approached they saw the nude body of a dead woman. At autopsy, it was discovered that she had died of gash wounds to the neck and had been the victim of a sexual assault. Police were later to learn that her death bore striking similarities to two other offenses some months earlier. Suspicion that a serial killer was at work proved to be well-founded.

Because of the high-profile nature of the case, many theories and rumors circulated. The suspect was first believed to be a white male driving a white pick-up truck. New evidence then pointed to a black man driving a Mitsubishi Mirage who was also wanted in connection with a rape. This suspect was Derrick Lee Todd.

Crystal Faye Todd Homicide

Crystal Faye Todd was a popular teenager at Conway High School, South Carolina. On the evening of her murder, Crystal had attended a birthday party for her grandmother in neighboring Toddsville. She left the party at 7 p.m. and got into her 1991 Celica, drove to a local mall, and left again at 9 p.m. to go to another party. Owing to a friend's curfew, she and her friend left the party, but Crystal's curfew was one hour after her friend's. When she failed to arrive home, her mother called 911 and was told it was not unusual for young girls not to come home.

The next day Crystal was still not home, and police officers from the local station visited her mother to get further details. Crystal's body was later discovered with a blood trail leading from the roadway into a ditch. There were also signs of a struggle. Her shirt was torn and her shirt and bra had been pulled up to expose her breasts. Her belt was undone and her jeans were pulled down. It appeared as though her throat had been cut, probably more than once, and there were multiple stab wounds all over the body, including the breasts and abdomen, and some of her organs protruded from a stomach wound.

Above Crystal Faye Todd was a well-liked senior at Conway High School.

INDUCTIVE REASONING: CRYSTAL FAYE TODD CASE PROFILE CHARACTERISTICS

1 Recklessness is probably a noted characteristic. We would expect that the offender transferred blood to his automobile after the crime.

2 He is probably episodically employed; he is not a businessman or a professional. He probably has trouble with policies and coworkers and consequently has had trouble with long-term employment. His performance, generally, at work, would be cyclical. He may work well one week and not so well the next. We would expect cyclical social performance as well; he may be nice one day, ornery the next. People who know him may say that one never knows what to expect from him.

3 He probably does not have a lot to make him attractive to peer females. For the most part, females from his peer group do not have a lot to do with him. He is not witty. He is not charming. He would probably be attractive to younger girls simply because he is older. Perhaps what he could offer peer females would be drugs or money (though it is not expected that he would have much money).

Police later arrested and charged Johnnie Kenneth Register II, a
neighbor and former boyfriend of Crystal's. He was 18 at the time
of the offense, was a pallbearer at the funeral, and often visited her
mother after her death. He was therefore not an obvious suspect at
first, but during DNA testing he displayed degrees of paranoia that
raised doubts, confirmed when the DNA results came through.

DEDUCTIVE PROFILING

Deductive profiles are more certain in their development of offender
characteristics, because in a deductive argument the conclusion *must*
be true *if* the premises are true. So, if one is careful to establish the
relevance and meaning of all premises on which the profile is based, then
any conclusions drawn from them will be accurate and true. As a general
rule, those who support the use of deduction will argue against the use
of pure induction in a profile because of the risk of error and the general

nature of inductive profiles. Having said that, deduction relies to some degree on induction, and this is where things tend to get confusing.

Deduction relies in part on knowledge built up inductively.

It would not be correct to argue that induction and deduction are opposing arguments. On the contrary, deduction relies in part on the knowledge that we have built up inductively through observation and experience. For this reason, an approach may not be entirely deductive (although an approach can be entirely inductive – see the discussion below on the scientific method).

Another way to characterize deduction is as *evidence-based* reasoning, because it is driven by the physical and behavioral evidence and not by generalizations about what offenders are *usually* like or *usually* do. That is to say, the final conclusion becomes a matter of certainty based on the way evidence is collected and interpreted, and the final conclusion is not argued on some possible outcome.

Scientific Method

In collecting and testing the evidence on which the deductive profile rests, another process becomes very important. This process is known as the scientific method. A cornerstone of the scientific method is falsification, which involves testing a theory against the established evidence with a view to proving these theories *wrong*.

The Scientific Method and Deduction

Brent Turvey addressed scientific method in his book *Criminal Profiling*, and his summary neatly explains not only the place of the scientific method, but also induction within a deductive method.

He states:

"The scientific method is a way of obtaining knowledge through a dynamic process of gathering information and testing, called experimentation. Experimentation involves both inductive and deductive reasoning. Inductively speaking, isolated facts are gathered and combine to form a general idea or hypothesis. Deductively speaking, generally accepted rules are used to form specific conclusions within the process. So in a science, induction is the beginning of reasoning, a place to start, and the formation of a deductively valid argument is the desired conclusion."

Hans Gross, who wrote what could be considered one of the first and most comprehensive textbooks on criminal investigation, comments:

> " We should not look for proofs of our suspicions in every piece of evidence, but proofs that our suspicions are not correct. If we seek to negative our suspicions in this way, then we are applying a scientific method and our work will be more complete. "

Risk Assessment

In performing a risk assessment of a particular victim, it would be usual to consider a number of features of the victim's overall occupational, social, and psychological circumstances. These may include their emotion and mood, their state of mind at the time of the offense, and their occupation, age, sex, race, and drug or alcohol usage. The idea is that some of these things are known to be general risk factors for certain offenses (such as age and sex in sexual assault), so these would be factors we understand to be generally true in crimes of this type. In assessing any case, these factors may contribute toward either the victim's lifestyle risk or their incident risk. So if a young female

---

DEDUCTIVE REASONING: MWIVANO KUPAZA CASE
PROFILE CHARACTERISTICS

This crime evidences an offender with medical knowledge. The basis for this opinion resides in consideration of the following items:

1 This victim was not dismembered with commonly associated chopping instruments such as a hatchet, cleaver, or machete applied to areas of bone (such as a butcher might use).

2 There is no evidence that a sawing instrument such as a hacksaw, band saw, skill saw, or radial saw was used.

3 There is evidence that the offender(s) separated the victim's head, arms, legs, and feet at their respective joints with the utmost deliberation, precision and care, using a very sharp cutting instrument not unlike a scalpel.

prostitute was found dead it may seem rational to argue that she was at high risk of being a victim of this type of crime. This would be an example of pure induction, and the limits of this approach are clear.

However, adopting a deductive approach providing us with a more comprehensive victimology, we may in fact discover that this victim lived with a room-mate who looked out for her, that she had a small, select group of clientele, all of whom are recorded in her address book, she takes self-defense classes, and does not abuse drugs or alcohol. This knowledge derived from a more thorough investigation into her background and stated deductively may in fact suggest that she is not high risk at all.

The Nature of Deductive Logic

One easy way to determine the nature of the logic used within a profile is to look for the supporting physical and behavioral evidence and its interpretation. As we've seen, an inductive profile is based on varying levels of statistical probability and the research on which they are based may occasionally be shown. In a deductive process, there will usually be an extensive analysis conducted to outline the interpretation of the evidence prior to the profile characteristics being offered, though supporting physical evidence may also be offered at the specific point the characteristic is argued.

Peter Kupaza

In July 1999, 25-year-old Mwivano Kupaza's dismembered body was found, with the parts distributed between several plastic bags that had been placed inside a duffel bag and dumped in the Wisconsin River. Her arms, legs, feet, and head had been separated by a razor-sharp cutting tool. A similarly sharp tool was used to remove the skin from her face, head, and neck. The disarticulation of the body and the removal of the skin proved to be a significant obstacle to the investigation, with the victim not being identified until February 2000.

The same month that the victim was recognized, another Tanzanian immigrant, the victim's cousin Peter Kupaza, was arrested for her murder. He had surgical skill from cutting up livestock in Tanzania, a fingerprint of the victim was found on his postal box, and a positive identification for biological fluids was made in his home. For the

Risk assessment

considers factors relating to the victim's occupational, social, and psychological circumstances. These can include the following:

1 Emotion, mood, and state of mind at the time of the offense
2 Occupation
3 Sex
4 Race
5 Drug or alcohol usage

TURVEY PROFILE FOR GENNA GAMBLE CASE

It is my opinion that this victim, Genna Gamble, was at a high overall risk of being the victim of a violent crime. The basis for my opinion on this issue resides in the consideration of the following items:

1 The victim was diagnosed with Oppositional Defiant Disorder. She was characterized by her therapist as exhibiting behavior which included the sudden loss of temper, deliberate antagonizing of others, refusal to obey parental instruction, and impulsivity.

2 The victim was known to have a low self-image, which would make her particularly susceptible to the approaches of certain types of sex offenders (those who use a con that involves flattery or the suggestion of acceptance).

3 The victim often spent time at locations socializing with age-inappropriate males, unsupervised by adults (the mall, Camelot & Funworks).

4 The victim was known to have socialized with a sex offender whose victims of choice included girls in Genna Gamble's age range, that were acquired at locations similar to the types that Genna Gamble frequented when unsupervised.

5 The victim was thought to have been likely to get into a car with someone whom she knew from Camelot (a video game parlor).

6 The victim's brother, Gerran Gamble, was known to have been dealing drugs, which he stored at their home.

first time in a US courtroom, an expert criminal profiler was allowed to testify about profiling during the guilt phase of a trial. (Experts often testify about profiling, but usually under the banner of some other form of evidence, since profiling is not typically allowed. See chapter 6 for more on the value of profiling in the courtroom.)

The Homicide of Genna Gamble

The naked body of Genna Lyn Gamble from Modesto, California, was found along Dry Creek, near Waterford, on October 14, 1995. Her stepfather, Douglas Mouser, was arrested and charged for the murder. The prosecution maintained that she had been killed in their Modesto home and then taken to the dump site. She had died from strangulation.

Michael Prodan, a Department of Justice profiler, testified for the prosecution in the case and it would appear that his profile evidence was given considerable weight. After a three-month trial and more than four years after her body was found, Douglas Mouser was found guilty of the murder of his step-daughter. This, despite the fact that there was only one (very weak) piece of evidence suggesting Mouser's guilt – the fact that a pattern on a seat belt in his car matched a pattern on her thigh. A host of experts, even one of the prosecution's own, concluded that the "match" of the mark on her thigh to the seat belt in the car had no basis. In answer to Prodan's testimony, the defense asked Brent Turvey to provide an analysis of his own. An excerpt of his victimology is presented above.

THE PROBLEMS WITH INDUCTION AND DEDUCTION

The fundamental differences between induction and deduction are relatively easy to understand, but a profiler using induction can pass off their profile deductively, misrepresenting the quality and soundness of their conclusions. The irony of this misunderstanding is that while this is the most basic difference between profilers and their respective abilities, it is also the most critical in terms of quality and how specific the profile will be to the current case.

Induction, while a component of a deductive method, is the most problematic form of reasoning in profiling. This is particularly true when it is employed in its pure form – that is, relying only on what is known though experience and research. On the other hand, deduction, while not providing the same volume of information, provides accuracy not possible through an inductive process. From a practical point of view, deduction is most relevant to a criminal investigation, especially should the profile be relied upon as a form of expert testimony in a court of law.

Below Armed with the technology to be able to compare DNA samples, investigators and juries can be much more certain about evidential links to suspects. In the Genna Gamble case, where DNA evidence was conspicuously absent, the decision rested on tenuous – and later discredited – evidence of a seat belt impression.

chapter 5

HOW USEFUL IS CRIMINAL PROFILNG?

What measure can we use to determine whether criminal profiling is any good, whether one profile is better than another, or whether the work of one individual profiler makes the grade? Studying profiling in live police investigations is hampered by the need for confidentiality that would block research, but mock scenarios are an unrealistic alternative. What has been done so far?

Opposite Profilers were criticized over the Waco case, where David Koresh and 85 cult followers died.

THE VALUE OF PROFILING

Criminal profilers have been shown to add immeasurably in some cases and in others to have done far more damage than good. Following is an analysis of the value of the science as it's developed so far.

STUDIES ON THE VALUE OF CRIMINAL PROFILING

Studies on the value of profiling fall roughly into one of the three following categories:

1 **Accuracy:** Where the ability of a profiler is measured against a case where the outcome is known, to see whether they can accurately identify the characteristics of the offender.
2 **Consumer satisfaction:** Assess profiling based on whether or not consumers of the profile are generally happy with the advice they receive and whether the advice assists the investigation.
3 **Comparative abilities:** Involves measuring the abilities between groups and is a form of accuracy study in which one group (for example, police detectives) is compared to other groups (for example, psychics, profilers, or lay people).

British Home Office Study

In the United Kingdom, the British Home Office conducted a study known as the *Coals to Newcastle Project* which was (in part) designed to test the accuracy of a profiler's opinions. All groups in the study were found to have an aggregate accuracy ratio of 2.2:1 meaning for every 2.2 correct points, there was 1 incorrect point. This suggests overall that the accuracy rate was about 66 percent. Looking at this a different way, profilers were wrong approximately one-third of the time.

FBI Study

The FBI claim to have an accuracy rate of 80 percent in their profiles, and in 1981, as part of its management practices, the FBI conducted a survey to gauge the value of service to their consumers. Overall,

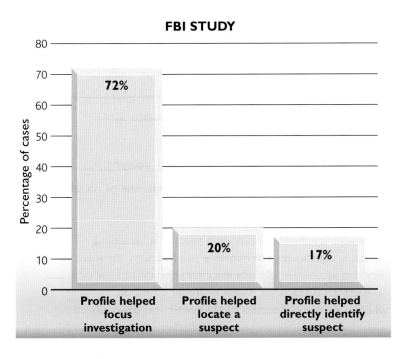

FBI STUDY

Percentage of cases

- 72% — Profile helped focus investigation
- 20% — Profile helped locate a suspect
- 17% — Profile helped directly identify suspect

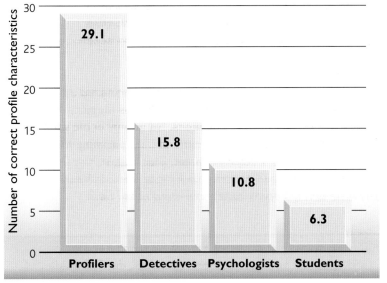

PINIZZOTTO/FINKEL STUDY 1990

Number of correct profile characteristics

- Profilers 29.1
- Detectives 15.8
- Psychologists 10.8
- Students 6.3

Left An FBI study was conducted in 1981 investigating the value of the work of profilers. In 88 cases solved where a criminal profiler had input, respondents said that the profile helped to focus the investigation in 72 percent of the cases, locate the suspect in 20 percent of the cases, and directly identify the suspect in 17 percent of the cases.

Below left The 1990 Pinizzotto/Finkel study looked at different processes used to arrive at a profile. Out of the four groups studied, profilers had the highest average number of correct profile characteristics, followed by detectives, pyschologists, and students.

192 end users were polled about the assistance received in 209 cases. Of these, 88 of the crimes had been solved and it was found that the profile helped focus the investigation in 72 percent of those cases. Also, the profile helped locate a suspect in 20 percent of the cases, and directly identified a suspect in 17 percent of cases. Essentially, the profile was found to be of no help to the same degree that it helped directly identify a suspect.

Process Studies

Anthony Pinizzotto teamed up with Normal Finkel in 1990 to conduct a study on the processes used by profilers, detectives, psychologists, and students in arriving at a profile. Out of the four groups, profilers had the highest average number of correct profile characteristics (29.1), with detectives coming in second (15.8), psychologists third (10.8), and students last (6.3). It was also found that the profilers wrote more detailed reports than the other groups, but there were mixed results about their ability to correctly identify offender characteristics.

Dutch Profiling Service Study

In the late 1980s, crime analysis became an important issue in the Netherlands and the Dutch police sent an officer to the FBI Academy for a one-year training course in Criminal Investigative Analysis. Upon his return, a new profiling unit made up of police and psychologists was opened that offered profiling services to police who requested help. To evaluate the use of the service, detailed interviews were conducted with 20 detective teams who employed their services. In total, there were 42 types of advice given to the teams, though there were only six complete profiles. Investigative suggestions were the most common form of advice, followed by personality assessments and crime assessments. Interview techniques and threat assessments were also given.

Of the total evaluations, two were viewed in a completely negative way. Out of the six actual profiles, the results were mixed. Two were judged as positive, three as intermediate, and one as negative. Without knowing more about how useful or in what context, judgment of the two positive and three intermediate assessments cannot be provided. No criminals were caught as a direct result of the profiles. Because of other restraints, the profiles weren't even used in four of the six cases.

Believing is Seeing

One Australian researcher, Richard Kocsis, has devoted a considerable amount of effort to studying the effectiveness of profilers versus other groups in the *Believing is Seeing* series of journal articles (in a similar way to the early studies of effectiveness). Another part of his research has been in gauging the credibility given to a profile by changing perceptions of who wrote it.

Police officers were given a profile and told it was either written by a professional profiler or by some unknown person. When evaluating the accuracy of the profile, the police officers consistently believed that the report of a "professional profiler" was more accurate, regardless of the content of the actual profiles.

In later additions to the *Believing is Seeing* series, the same thing was studied using a non-police sample. In all cases, the perceived accuracy for the "professional profiler" was higher than the non-professional profiler. Those people who held positive attitudes toward profiling as a useful means of understanding information to solve crimes also scored higher on their estimated accuracy than the other groups. These studies suggest that over and above the limitations of determining actual accuracy, it may be possible to

Below left Gary Ridgway, the "Green River serial killer," murdered 48 women over a 20-year period. FBI profiler John Douglas devised the profile which eventually led to Ridgway's capture.

Below right Richard Trenton Chase was convicted in 1979 of six counts of murder. The profile used in the investigation identified the offender as a white male in his mid-20s, under-nourished, disorganized, and impulsive, with a history of mental illness and/or drug use. Chase fit the profile exactly.

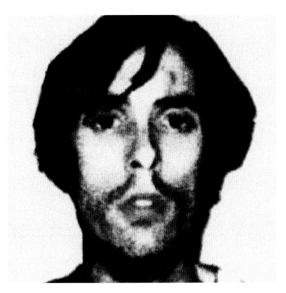

Below left Ukrainian serial killer Andrei Chikatilo confessed to 55 counts of murder. It is arguable whether the profile drawn up by Viktor Burakov did anything to help focus police investigation.

Below right Wayne B. Williams was convicted of the Atlanta child murders in the late 1970s. Chet Dettlinger discovered a social and geographic pattern between the victims. During the peak of the murders, he was able to predict with a degree of accuracy where victims would disappear and be found.

manipulate a person's perception of the usefulness and accuracy of a profile.

PROBLEMS WITH ACCURACY

Even though it might sound like a good idea to judge a profiler's competence by the accuracy of their profiles, the reality doesn't match up to the expectation. This occurs for a number of reasons. First, the way in which the profile and the characteristics of the offender are cross-checked can be very subjective and might depend very heavily on the method used to match the characteristics of the suspect to the profile. Secondly, the accuracy (or perceived accuracy) of a profile may be less significant than the assistance it provides. What's more, we might have two profiles by two different profilers in two different cases, with an offender caught in the first case but not the second. Does the first profiler have the right to claim greater accuracy because they have a result and a conviction, even though the second profile may be more accurate if the offender is eventually caught?

Some criminal profilers boldly claim that accuracy equals usefulness: If their profile was right it must have been useful. This thinking is flawed and assumes the profile was used in the investigation. Others

argue that if their work was not accurate, then they wouldn't get so many calls for assistance; however, a profile may be called on as a last act of desperation in a high-profile case where public and political pressure forces investigators to try something unconventional. It may, in fact, have nothing to do with the esteem in which the profiler is held.

Perhaps more of a problem is the fact that some profiles are so vague and general they are virtually useless. Any profile can claim that an offender is a white male, aged 17 to 24 and be right in most offenses, but these three features alone do little to explain the way this offender might differ from any other. In *Offender Profiling and Crime Analysis,* Peter Ainsworth gives a very effective similar example:

> " One profiler may, for instance, be quite specific in stating that an attacker is about 20 years of age and lives within a 100-yard radius of where the attack took place. By contrast, another profiler might be much more vague, putting an attacker's age at between 18 and 40 and stating that he probably lives in the (same) large town as the victim. Technically, both of these profiles might prove to be 'accurate' yet their relative utility is very different. "

Below left Richard Speck, murderer of eight Chicago nurses in 1966. A sociopath, he murdered the women with apparently little motive. A witness survived the crime, giving a vital description which, combined with some geographic profiling, led to his apprehension.

Below right John Wayne Gacy was arrested in December 1978 on 33 charges of murder. Criminologist Robert Ressler came to the case after Gacy was identified as a suspect but helped flesh out the psychological profile that aided the prosecution.

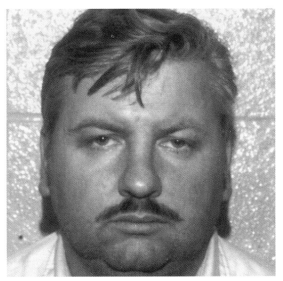

- Logic difficult to reproduce
- Theory upon which method is based may be questionable

PROBLEMS WITH CIA

- Poor inter-rater reliability
- Organized/disorganized characteristics not given different weighting
- Organized offender may leave disorganized crime scene
- Concept of disorganized offender dubious

The profiler should always be aware of the level of investigative relevance their profiles have. Without this, criminal profiling will find it difficult to gain any ground.

CRITIQUES OF THE INDIVIDUAL METHODS

The individual methods described in chapter 3 all have positive features, but they also have bad points. It stands to reason that the oldest and most prevalent method (CIA) is the one that has been discussed and criticized the most. As a general rule, inductive methods are cited as having the most problems (though, keep in mind the inductive methods are also the greatest in number).

Diagnostic Evaluations

Because of the many different approaches a psychologist or psychiatrist might take in profiling an offender, the diagnostic evaluation does not actually represent a single method, but is a general term for assessments by mental health professionals. These differences mean that the logic used can be difficult to reproduce and study, or the theory or method it is based on may be questionable. Additionally, owing to the fact that most psychologists aren't experienced in criminal investigations, the advice given is not always entirely relevant to police investigations. This might include things like the inner workings of an offender's mental processes, the offender's developmental history, or their psychosexual development, all of which may be difficult to identify in a suspect.

Criminal Investigative Analysis

CIA is the most critiqued method of profiling. Even the original study on which the method was based was heavily criticized, with reviewers noting problems, mostly based on the statistical procedures used. Agents conducting the interviews were left to decide which of the groups the offender they were interviewing belonged to, and they didn't later come together to see if their classifications were correct. (In statistical terms, this is referred to as **inter-rater reliability** and is very important.) Further, there is no specific discussion on whether any of the elements of the organized or disorganized approach are given greater weight, or how specific crime scene characteristics match up against offender characteristics.

Brent Turvey and David Canter provide the most damning reviews of this approach, with Turvey focusing on the method's practical side, and Canter critiquing it from the underlying theory. Turvey's concern is that there are a number of situations where an organized offender will leave a disorganized crime scene, affecting the ability of the profiler to accurately identify offender characteristics. These situations include:

1 Anger-retaliatory offenders not suffering from mental illness.
2 Domestic violence-related offenses (where emotions and anger usually run high).
3 Staged offenses.
4 Interrupted offenses where an offender is unable to complete their crime.
5 Offenses involving controlled substances (including "hard" drugs such as cocaine, but also socially accepted drugs such as alcohol).

In testing the theory of the model, Canter notes that "despite weaknesses in the organized/disorganized classification of serial killers, it is drawn on for 'offender profiles,' theories of offending, and in murder trials." Because of the reliance on this model, Canter set about verifying its foundations. In a recent study, Canter and his colleagues found little support in a sample of US serial killers, with the results indicating no subset of offenders suggested by the dichotomy, though they did find a subset of organized features that were typical of most serial killers. The disorganized features are much rarer, though, and do not reflect a distinct type. Canter's study raises serious concerns about this particular approach and its worth.

Investigative Psychology

While sharing some similarities with other inductive methods, IP uses data from much broader samples, and so the research is more relevant to the broader population, though this doesn't mean that IP has escaped criticism. In analyzing an offender's behavior, Canter uses a statistical technique known as Smallest Space Analysis (SSA). This provides a graphical representation of the relationship between variables, with those variables placed closer together on the plot being more related, while those further apart are less related. In

PROBLEM WITH INVESTIGATIVE PSYCHOLOGY
- Similar behaviors across crimes are grouped as related when motive might differ entirely

Above and opposite

Computer-generated maps developed by Dr. Kim Rossmo's team to help pinpoint probable locations for next likely attacks.

using the plot to determine common (or "core") and distinguishing characteristics, it may be possible to confuse two features of an offense as related, because the motive for the behavior is either assumed or ignored.

For example, during one offense a rapist might bite the breast of the victim for the purpose of sexual gratification. A different offender might bite the breast of the victim because of an over-zealous attempt at "foreplay." The motivation for the two behaviors is different, but because the behavior is the same they may be clustered in a similar way on the plot. Also, the grouping of certain variables might occur, not because those variables are related, but because they are not related to any other variables.

Geographic Profiling

Although the computational basis of geographic profiling is well established, Rossmo himself notes an element of subjectivity in determining which crime sites are useful in predicting an offender's

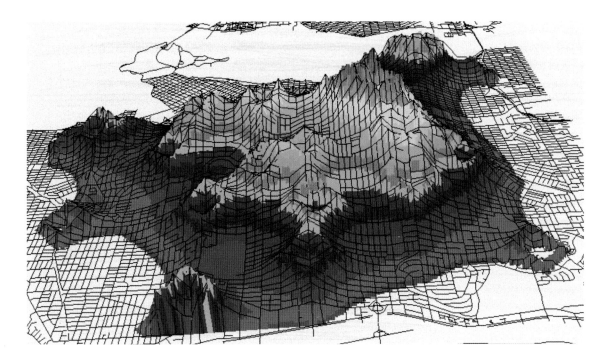

residence. Like other inductive methods, geographic profiling is probabilistic and can only provide general ideas about an offender's behavior arising from the study of past similar offenders. Turvey raises seven concerns about geographic profiling:

1 This approach ignores the fundamentals of behavior analysis; it takes a single behavior and interprets it outside its context.
2 Although Rossmo notes that this method should be used only in conjunction with a full psychological profile, there have been instances where a geoprofile has been completed without this.
3 The result of ignoring the overall behavioral context in which an offense occurs means that geographic profiling cannot differentiate between two or more offenders operating in the same area.
4 The method assumes that all cases have been linked and does not check whether this is in fact the case.
5 The method assumes that offenders live near or within easy reach of their offense area.

PROBLEM WITH GEOGRAPHIC PROFILING

- Geoprofiling is probabilistic and can only provide general suggestions for an offender's behavior based on past similar offenders

PROBLEMS WITH BEA
- Premises must be clearly established before any conclusions drawn
- Time-consuming – no "quick fix" – but most accurate

6 The doctoral dissertation on which the method is based outlines the flaws in current serial murder research but then goes on to rely on this same flawed research.

7 The technology used in the calculations is impressive but can only go so far. Any final assessment must be done by an analyst.

Behavioral Evidence Analysis

As noted, BEA is the most recent addition to profiling. There are few criticisms of the method, and those criticisms that do exist are easily controlled. With a deductive method, the conclusions must be true if the premises are true, and Michael McGrath notes that the profiler may be wrong if the premises on which they base the profile are also wrong. While this can be a problem, it is more of a general caution to those using a deductive method that they must establish the premises before drawing any conclusions from them.

Ronald and Steven Holmes, authors of *Profiling Violent Crimes*, suggest that "much care is taken from the examination of forensic reports, victimology, and so forth and the report will take much longer to develop using this approach." While not a criticism *per se*, the consumer is warned that a deductive profile is not a quick fix, and any analysis may take time to complete.

WHEN PROFILING CAUSES HARM

Most profilers are quick to shout about their successes, but they are equally quick to conceal their failures. This may particularly be the case when the failure is high-profile, or when a well-known organization is involved. In all cases, profilers may fall into a blame game, trying to implicate others in their errors, or simply refuse to take responsibility for their own work. Information about failures in criminal profiling is plentiful if you know where to look: The results of these failures are catastrophic.

The USS Iowa Incident

Early one morning in April 1989, Turret Two on board the USS Iowa blew up, killing 47 of the crewman and sending shockwaves through the US Navy that would reverberate for years to come. The explosion and the subsequent investigation revealed dangerous practices,

incompetence, cover-ups, and investigative failures, only some of which were related to the explosion and deaths. Given the magnitude of the disaster, the Navy decided to consult with agents from the FBI's Behavioral Sciences Unit, to gain some insight into what they believed were the suicidal actions of one of the ship's crew, Gunner's Mate Clayton Hartwig.

While the "equivocal death analysis" (or "EDA" – essentially a profile on a deceased person) conducted by the FBI was not responsible for initially blaming Hartwig and painting him as a depressive, suicidal homosexual, it was most certainly responsible for cementing this in the minds of investigators and the Naval executive. What followed was both a synergy of bad judgment and a self-fulfilling prophecy: investigators from the Naval Investigative Service (NIS) suggested Hartwig's guilt from the onset, providing information to the FBI profilers to this effect, and this came back to them in the form a profile.

With regards to the EDA, a report of the Investigations Subcommittee of the Committee on Armed Services House of Representatives noted two important issues with the FBI's analysis:

1 The procedures the FBI used in preparing the EDA were inadequate and unprofessional. As a matter of policy, the analysts do not state the speculative nature of their analyses. Moreover, the parameters that the FBI agents used, either

Above Aerial view of the battleship USS Iowa BB-61 firing her guns while at sea in the late 1980s. Following the incident on board in 1989, the explosion was attributed to the intentional suicidal acts of Gunner's Mate Clayton Hartwig, a conclusion supported primarily by an "equivocal death analysis" conducted by the FBI.

Right Memorial service for the 47 crewmen killed in the explosion on board the USS Iowa in April 1989. Gunner's Mate Clayton Hartwig was blamed for the explosion; however, the investigation into the incident was found to be both inadequate and unprofessional as the reports were highly speculative and biased.

provided to them or chosen by them, biased their results toward only one of three deleterious conclusions. Further biasing their conclusions, the agents relied on insufficient and sometimes suspect evidence. The FBI agents' EDA was invalidated by 10 of 14 professional psychologists and psychiatrists, heavily criticized even by those professionals who found the Hartwig possibility plausible.

2 The FBI analysis gave the Navy false confidence in the validity of the FBI's work. If the Navy had relied solely on the work of NIS's own staff psychologist – which emphasized that such psychological autopsies are by definition "speculative" – the Navy would likely not have found itself so committed to the Hartwig thesis.

Despite the questionable nature of the whole EDA process, the analysis was still given significant airplay during the investigation. In later testimony, it was revealed that this same process had been employed in at least 50 cases – but that a "satisfactory result" had been obtained in only three. Much worse, it would appear that all of those involved in the investigation – the Naval Investigative Service, the FBI, and to some degree the Navy themselves – had been working from the same page: Clayton Hartwig was a suicidal homosexual.

In his book *A Glimpse of Hell*, retired naval officer Charles Thompson is very critical of the FBI and the case in general. Thompson tells how the FBI profilers, Roy Hazelwood and Richard Ault, had a "rough time" when they appeared before the Senate Armed Services Committee. In defending their analysis, the agents claimed to possess the depth of knowledge and experience necessary to make psychological determinations about criminal suspects, knowledge which the academic community would not have.

The following concerns were also raised about Hartwig's guilt and the conclusions in their profile:

1 Richard Ault admitted that the Navy had only provided him with fragments of the evidence assembled against Hartwig.
2 Ault was asked who wrote the poem "Disposable Heroes," a key piece of evidence on which Hartwig's alleged homosexuality hinged, and he didn't know.
3 Asked whether the agents were aware that another gunner's mate told Admiral Milligan that another sailor had written the poem, Hazelwood stated this was immaterial as Hartwig had the potential to see it.
4 The agents were asked if they were aware that David Smith had recanted the testimony used in their EDA, and they claimed they weren't sure what he had recanted.
5 The agents had relied entirely on the information provided to them by the NIS and had not done any interviews themselves.
6 When asked if Ault had any "hard evidence, any evidence that would support the idea that Hartwig carried out this act," he responded, "No sir . . . this opinion that we submitted is based on half scientific, half art form."

The impact that the "suicidal homosexual" label had not only on the memory of Hartwig but on his family must also be considered. In a critical review of the FBI's practices in the Iowa investigation, the American Psychological Association suggests that "the EDA conducted by the FBI led the navy to conclude that Clayton Hartwig was responsible for a disastrous explosion, a conclusion with substantial implications on a number of fronts." These include:

1 On a personal level Hartwig's own reputation and that of his family and friends were affected by the controversy.
2 The FBI-Navy findings could potentially have influenced decisions regarding benefits due to Hartwig's family or other beneficiaries (for example, life insurance).
3 The Navy's findings could also potentially affect future decisions regarding benefits to families of other sailors.

The reaction of the media to the testimony of the two "mindhunters" was extremely negative. One column in the *New York Daily News* read: "Deep within the FBI there exists a unit of people who – without ever talking to you or anyone who knows you – are prepared to go into court and testify that you are a homicidal maniac."

Right David Koresh, cult leader of the Branch Davidian sect, died when federal law enforcement officers stormed the compound to end the 51-day siege at the Waco ranch in Texas. He was profiled as a man who had a great amount of power to suggest to his followers that an attack was coming and they were going to have to defend themselves. When the compound was stormed, the Branch Davidians saw Koresh's prophecies coming true.

Waco, Texas

In April 1993, a 51-day siege at the Branch Davidian Compound at Mount Carmel, Texas, ended with the death of David Koresh and 85 of his followers (the actual number of deaths changes depending on the source) including men, women, and children. All of these people died as a result of actions of federal law enforcement: some from a fire; some were shot; others perhaps took their own lives. While there is evidence not all died directly at the agents' hands, if not for the siege, these people, in all likelihood, would still be alive.

Besides problems with the original warrants obtained by law enforcement officers and the media attention paid to the Branch Davidians, the fiery end that the group members met can, in a considerable way, be attributed to the work of a profiler advising on the case. Even without the benefit of hindsight, the actual end of the Branch Davidians, if not directly foreseeable, was at least one of a number of scenarios that had been considered. In the profile of Koresh it was acknowledged that "In traditional hostage situations a strategy which has been successful has been negotiation coupled with ever increasing tactical presence. In this situation, however, it is believed this strategy, if carried to excess, could eventually be counterproductive and could result in loss of life."

So, as two branches of the federal government closed in, it would appear that, to the Davidians at least, the prophecies of their leader

Above Many members of the sect died from asphyxiation as fire raced through the compound. Others, mostly women and children who huddled under wet blankets in a concrete chamber, were fatally injured when debris collapsed on them during the fire. Still others were shot in apparent mercy killings. The pattern of most of the bodies was not consistent with a theory of mass suicide.

David Koresh were coming true. However, instead of trying to defuse the situation, pressure from federal law enforcement was stepped up. This despite a warning that "as of March 5, 1993, Koresh is still able to convince his followers that the end is near and, as he predicted, their enemies will surround them and kill them."

This wasn't the only warning in the profile about the group's belief that an armed presence may signify something destructive. It was further noted that "Every time his followers sense movement of tactical personnel Koresh validates his prophetic warnings that an attack is forthcoming and they are going to have to defend themselves. According to his teachings, if they die defending their faith, they will be saved."

It would appear then that the blunder wasn't a mere oversight, and that those acting in an advisory role were well aware of the social and religious environment in play at Waco. Unfortunately, this knowledge didn't do much good at the end of the day.

Originally taking the stance that the Branch Davidians were a peaceful religious group, Peter Smerick of the Behavioral Sciences Unit soon changed his position as a result of the pressure he felt from his superiors. According to an article in the *New York Times* in 1995, Smerick was a senior agent from the FBI's Behavioral Science Center in Quantico and at Waco during the crucial period of March 2–17, when the FBI's strategy was being developed. Smerick's written profiles of Koresh advised FBI tacticians and negotiators to out-wait Koresh. Smerick warned that Koresh might otherwise order a mass suicide if he felt he was being threatened. He advised that taking a bullish strategy, "if carried to excess, could eventually be counterproductive and could result in loss of life."

FBI officials didn't heed Smerick's warning. In fact, they even tried to get Smerick to change it.

Smerick was quoted as saying that FBI officials had complained that the first four memos he had written advising they take a cautious approach "were tying their hands." The senior agents "didn't want

---

Opposite The aftermath of the Waco siege at the Branch Davidian cult compound in Texas. Eight survivors were convicted on charges ranging from voluntary manslaughter to weapons violations, most of whom were sentenced to 40 years in prison.

a memo coming up [to FBI headquartes] saying the same thing."
The journalist of the *New York Times* article reported that FBI inter-
mediaries made it clear to Smerick in several phone conversations on
March 9 that Smerick should discuss the contents of his memos with
FBI headquarters before writing any further advice.

Smerick realized his views were being "sanitized."

" You don't have to be hit with a two-by-four to get the message they want their own
input on memos coming up, " Smerick said.

In Smerick's next memo, on March 9, he adopted a "get-tough"
approach, downplaying caution. The memo advised that, since
negotiations had had limited success, "other measures" should be
employed. Such measures might include switching on and off the
utilities, moving FBI agents and equipments closer to the house and
cutting off all negotiations.

It seemed then, that the proposed peaceful "wait and see"
approach was not at all favorable to the FBI brass who were
ultimately in charge of the situation.

One could argue that Smerick's position about the pressure was
merely an attempt to save his own reputation and career, though his
concern about the pressure he felt from above was later corroborated
by his supervisor at the time, John Douglas.

Douglas was a 25-year veteran of the FBI and was chief of the
investigative support unit that supplied negotiators for the FBI
operation. It was later reported in The *New York Times* that
Douglas was among those negotiators who felt intense pressure to
keep quiet about information given to him from his team of criminal
profilers, psychologists and analysts. He is quoted as claiming that
his group clashed several times with the hostage rescue team, the
more powerful tactical group, which wanted active results and
dismissed the scientists.

" I felt I had no choice but to keep my mouth shut or I'd be rustling
cattle somewhere, " Douglas said.

Turvey is critical of the actions of the profilers in this case. In the second edition of his text he notes:

> According to both Mr. Smerick and Mr. Douglas, Attorney General Janet Reno acted on information provided by Mr. Smerick, who agreed to change his last report under pressure from Mr. Douglas (who was under pressure from his bosses at the FBI) to favor a breach at Waco.
>
> According to their own accounts, Mr. Douglas and Mr. Smerick agreed to alter their professional expert opinions as criminal profilers regarding Waco to favor those of their supervisors, for fear of losing their jobs, or other sanctions. This is a decision that both understood could cost lives.

The Murder of Rachel Nickell

In July 1992, 23-year-old Rachel Nickell and her two-year-old son, Alex, went for a walk on Wimbledon Common in the United Kingdom. Nickell was stabbed 49 times in front of her son, whose life was spared. In the investigation that ensued, police would turn to well-known psychologist, Paul Britton, in their hunt for the killer. The case became the country's most publicized of the year, and the implications of the profiler's involvement are wide-ranging.

Britton's profile was uncanny in describing Colin Stagg, who had come to the attention of police during their inquiries. Despite the fact there was no actual evidence linking him to the crime, he became the prime suspect and later focus of entrapment. In order to secure

Right Rachel Nickell was murdered in front of her two-year-old son on Wimbledon Common, London, in 1992.

- Assumption that the scrap of paper found placed on Rachel Nickell's forehead was part of a bizarre ritualistic act by the killer.

A year following the murder, the police discovered this had instead been the act of an uncomprehending toddler, placing a "plaster" on his mother's forehead in an attempt to make her better.

evidence about what police felt could only have been Stagg's guilt, they employed Britton in an advisory role, further enlisting the help of an attractive 33-year-old officer to engage in suggestive correspondence with Stagg. This police officer is known only as "Lizzie James."

In the *The Journal of Forensic Science*, Edwards gives the following account of the communications between Stagg and "James," and Britton's assessment of it:

" Through an attractive blonde undercover policewoman, the psychologist initiated an eight months' liaison with the 31-year-old Stagg in which she shared violent sexual fantasies, confessed to the ritual sexual murder of a baby and a young woman, and egged him on to match her stories; even telling him that she wished he were Nickell's murderer . . . Stagg never claimed credit for the killing, but from 700 pages of letters and transcribed telephone conversations and public meetings, the psychologist [Paul Britton] concluded that Stagg's fantasies, modelled upon information fed to him by those familiar with the details of the crime, revealed unique knowledge of the crime scene which could only be known by the murderer. "

Stagg was tried in open court at the Old Bailey. His defense quickly pointed out that Stagg hadn't even made good guesses – he didn't know the location of the crime and had incorrectly assumed that the victim had been raped.

In court, Justice Ognall strongly condemned the "'femme fatale' police operation" led by psychologist Paul Britton, also commenting on the involvement of the profiler and the evidence he offered. He described the investigation as "thoroughly reprehensible" and ruled that "a careful appraisal of the material demonstrates a skilful and sustained enterprise to manipulate the accused, sometimes subtly, sometimes blatantly."

It would seem that Stagg was not the only victim in this case. After the trial, "Lizzie James" took 18 months of sick leave for post traumatic stress disorder, eventually retiring from the police force in 1998. She was also paid £125,000 (US$235,000) in compensation. This was not to be the end of it though, with Britton himself being taken to task over his opinions. A report in the *Western Daily Press* in 2002 describes how:

> " Britain's top criminal profiler and the man dubbed the real life Cracker was yesterday fighting to save his career before a disciplinary tribunal . . . Britton, believed to be the inspiration behind Robbie Coltrane's popular TV character, built up a profile of the killer who savagely murdered the pretty 23-year-old on Wimbledon Common, and told police it matched Colin Stagg's personality.
>
> The ruse backfired spectacularly and eventually led to the collapse of Stagg's trial at the Old Bailey. The police tactics were criticized by the judge in the Stagg case and the ensuing scandal led to many people questioning the use of criminal profilers. The society will now consider allegations of professional misconduct against Mr. Britton . . .
>
> And it will decide whether full disciplinary proceedings can be brought against Mr. Britton for his involvement in the murder inquiry. Colin Stagg has always claimed that Britton's part in the police investigation led detectives to using the discredited honey trap ploy. And he has campaigned for almost eight years for Britton to be disciplined over his role in the whole affair. "

In essence, instead of maintaining his impartiality as a consultant, Britton identified with the role of an advocate, attempting to help police not only catch their man, but also assisting in the collection of evidence, and the subsequent prosecution.

The judge, concerned about police tactics and the profiler's involvement in this, dismissed the case against Stagg noting "nobody questions that in certain cases the assistance of a psychologist of that kind can prove a useful tool. But the police went further . . . there can be no doubt that the accused was the subject of deliberate and sustained entrapment and that thereafter his responses, including the expression of his fantasies were the subject of subtle but constant effective manipulation by Lizzie James, designed to extract from him material (a) consistent with Mr Britton's profile and (b) hopefully a confession."

PROCEDURAL MISTAKES

- A Photofit of a suspect was released following Rachel Nickell's murder.

Colin Stagg maintains: "The only real reason I was arrested was that I had a passing resemblance to a Photofit description of one of many men seen on the Common."

chapter 6

PROFILERS IN THE COURTROOM

The testimony of experts in criminal and civil trials forms a complex but important part of our legal system. As science and scientific procedures advance, and new ones develop, the advice of experts becomes increasingly crucial. Their role is to present information to the court in simple and accessible language, so that the true meaning of the evidence is clear to judge and jury.

Opposite Dr. Samuel Sheppard appealed against his murder conviction but questionable expert evidence undermined his case.

EXPERT EVIDENCE

Despite a number of significant advances in theory and application in recent years, profiling has still not been widely accepted in the legal and scientific communities.

The reason that the field of criminal profiling has remained largely unaccepted is due to fragmentation in the profiling community, differences in profiling processes, conflict between members and groups in the community, and the lack of a database from which to draw information on crime types. Despite the power of the deductive method, many courts in their approach to profiling also seem to prefer inductive methods. There are many methods and many practitioners, and not all of them agree about what is best or appropriate. For these and other reasons, profiling hasn't yet received much airplay as expert evidence in court.

In this chapter we look at various rules relating to expert evidence that is given in court and the variety of ways in which a profiler may come to be considered an expert. These include the **Frye** and **Daubert rules** of evidence operating in the United States, and a detailed examination of the rules of expert evidence in Australia.

The general theme of the rules that govern US and Australian evidence is adopted in most legal systems throughout the world. For example, experts are not usually allowed to testify directly to someone's guilt or innocence (called the **ultimate issue rule**) – there must be some factual basis on which their opinion is made (called the **factual basis rule**), and the area in which the expert is testifying must be well-regarded in the scientific community to which it belongs. So, while the following legal discussions might be country-specific, their implications are universal. A selection of case studies where profilers have been allowed to testify as experts are used to demonstrate these rules.

FRYE AND DAUBERT RULES

In the United States, two rules have had the most impact on the presentation of expert evidence. The first is known as the **Frye rule**, from the case Frye v United States, and came about in 1923. The District

FRYE RULE

The Frye rule calls into question whether or not the field in which the expert is testifying is generally accepted by a considerable proportion of its scientific community.

Court of Columbia rejected evidence on the so-called "lie detector test" (polygraph) based on the lack of scientific agreement on the use of the polygraph. Frye has since become a standard for determining the admissibility of scientific evidence and tests. The Court noted:

> Just when a scientific principle or discovery crosses the line between the experimental and demonstrable stages is difficult to define. Somewhere in the twilight zone the evidential force of the principle must be recognized, and while the courts will go a long way in admitting expert testimony deduced from a well recognized scientific principle or discovery, the thing from which the deduction is made must be sufficiently established to have gained general acceptance in the particular field to which it belongs.

Above The lie detector test as it was in the 1950s. Here, Nate Zusman takes a polygraph as part of an investigation into corruption. Zusman owned a nightclub in Portland, Oregon, which was being investigated for being a gambling den. Zusman admitted paying money to Portland police.

The essence of Frye is whether or not the field in which the expert is testifying is *generally accepted* by a considerable proportion of its scientific community. Anyone wanting to present evidence under Frye must present to the court a number of experts who can testify that the procedure is accepted in that professional community. The criminal profiling profession may have difficulty passing muster under Frye because of the disagreement between profilers on which approach is the best.

On the other hand, when seeing if a field meets the criteria for acceptance, the courts have often looked at the amount of literature (academically reviewed journal articles and texts) that has been published on the subject. This would probably be one of profiling's strongest areas with a wide variety of material available.

DNA Evidence Originally Rejected

Interestingly, DNA evidence, which has since become a well-established form of evidence, was originally not allowed in a 1987 prosecution because at that point in time it could not pass the Frye test. DNA had previously been allowed in some courts, but what was known about it was deemed questionable until it received general acceptance from the scientific community.

Beyond Frye

Later, in 1993, the US Supreme Court established Daubert v Merrell Dow Pharmaceuticals. They felt that the court's decision in Frye was not an absolute prerequisite for the admissibility of scientific evidence under the Federal Rules of Evidence. The Frye standard was not friendly to new or novel forms of evidence, even though they might be entirely logical and reliable. Because of this, any new procedure that may have assisted the court in understanding certain evidence would probably not have been allowed, simply because it hadn't been around long enough to become "generally accepted."

The Daubert Rule

The Daubert rule takes a more relaxed approach than the Frye rule. It allows judges to become gatekeepers of their own courtroom, dictating on a case-by-case basis the "relevance" and "reliability"

DAUBERT RULE

Under the Daubert rule, judges can determine the relevance and reliability of testimony and therefore deem it admissable or inadmissable.

of testimony. Even though the court emphasized flexibility, they also offered some guidelines which include:

1 Whether the technique or theory can be (and has been) tested.
2 Whether the technique or theory has been subject to peer review and publication.
3 The technique's rate of error.
4 Existence and maintenance of standards controlling the technique's operation.
5 Whether the scientific theory or method has attracted widespread acceptance within a relevant scientific community.

These guidelines do not, as a general rule, fare well for the acceptance of profiling as expert testimony. But consider the points

ISSUES SURROUNDING ADMISSABILITY OF PROFILING EVIDENCE

1 Given the number of profiling approaches and the lack of one unified method, testing the theories of profiling might be difficult. Even though a number of research studies have been conducted into its effectiveness, these may not apply across the board to all practitioners, or to newly evolving methods.

2 Despite the fact that profiling is quite new, having developed over the last three decades, there is a fair amount of literature that is peer-reviewed and published.

3 As noted in chapter 5, studies into the effectiveness of profiling are often inconsistent at best, and the rate of error with many methods is quite high (ranging between 30 percent and 60 percent inaccurate).

4 At this point in time, there are few bodies or groups that govern the behavior of profilers. In the United

Kingdom, the Association of Chief Police Officers keeps a list of those who are qualified by their standards, with some other profilers having codes of conduct relevant to their professional trades (for example, a psychologist would be governed by the state or federal group overseeing this discipline). Thus far, only the Academy of Behavioral Profiling has put forward a set of ethical guidelines for their members that are directly related to criminal profiling. Overall, there is no one group setting universal standards to bind profilers.

5 From a historical and practical perspective, this is an interesting time in profiling with some of the early critiques being addressed, and newer methods challenging older ones that are insufficient. Despite this, we are still a long way from widespread acceptance within the relevant scientific community.

illustrated in the box on page 143; these issues need to be considered when making a decision whether or not to admit such testimony in light of Daubert.

Another adaptation to Daubert came along in 1999 with Kumho Tire Company Limited v Carmichael where the judge ruled that the gatekeeping role applied not only to scientific evidence, but also to technical and other specialized knowledge.

RULES OF EXPERT EVIDENCE

In Australia, there are five rules of evidence that are used to determine if both an expert and an area are deemed to be court-worthy. Despite these rules being specific to this country, they are relevant to most legal systems which operate under similar rules.

EXPERTISE RULE

The expert must be recognized as such.

1. Expertise Rule

This rule is quite straightforward and states that the expert must be considered an expert in their field. They do not have to be the leading practitioner, but they must have knowledge better than most. John Thornton, a forensic scientist in the United States, summarizes the general feeling of this rule as "when the liberty of an individual may depend in part on physical evidence it is not unreasonable to ask that the expert witnesses who are called upon to testify, either against the defendant or on his behalf, know what they are doing."

The information on what education, training, and experience you need to be able to call yourself a profiler is scarce, though some suggest a minimum level of training in the behavioral and forensic sciences that can be complemented by practical experience dealing with offenders.

AREA OF EXPERTISE RULE

An expert may testify only in an area that belongs to a formal sphere of knowledge and is therefore able to be evaluated.

2. Area of Expertise Rule

This rule states that an expert cannot testify in an area that does not belong to a formal sphere of knowledge since it must be possible to evaluate its theoretical and practical foundations. Only lately has a standard of workmanship come to profiling, and our ability to compel others to conform to these standards is still poor. As with guideline number four for the Daubert rule, establishing professional organizations may go a long way toward helping profiling gain recognition as an area of expertise.

3. Factual Basis Rule

As the name implies, there should be some factual basis on which to support the evidence. This rule is not exclusionary like the other rules, but dictates the strength given by the court to any conclusions offered. In some cases, the court may allow expert evidence even if the factual basis of the evidence has not been established, provided that after the evidence is given the facts on which it is based are proven.

Because a criminal profile relies on other evidence, such as crime-scene photographs, investigative reports, autopsy documentation, and witness reports, the weight given to the profile can only be as strong as other evidence it is based on. The quality of conclusions can then be judged by how much those conclusions relied on the evidence and the interpretation of that evidence.

4. Common Knowledge Rule

Because expert evidence is sometimes prejudicial, the court does not usually allow an expert to state something it considers to be within the jury's existing knowledge. It is unnecessary to have a profiler testify that "most crime is committed by males" because this is not something requiring specialist knowledge, though they may be allowed to give evidence that a crime was staged and what suggests such a conclusion.

Most aspects of a criminal profile require special knowledge that falls outside of the common knowledge of the juror. For example, most jurors wouldn't have difficulty understanding the characteristics of a domestic murder, as these are the most common type. The jurors may, however, find it difficult to make an assessment of a sexually sadistic murderer and their motivation, as these aren't as common (and thankfully not within the realm of experience of your "average" citizen).

5. Ultimate Issue Rule

The Ultimate Issue Rule refers to guilt or innocence, and an expert must not come to conclusions that suggest the responsibility of the person on trial one way or the other. This is not the expert's job in any way, but a decision that should be left up to the jury (or in some cases the judge).

FACTUAL BASIS RULE
There must be some factual basis to support the evidence.

COMMON KNOWLEDGE RULE
The expert may not state something considered to be common knowledge.

ULTIMATE ISSUE RULE
The expert must not make conclusions regarding guilt or innocence.

DNA EVIDENCE AND THE ULTIMATE ISSUE RULE

DNA is one form of evidence that has proved challenging. Experts frequently testify to the link between a sample taken from a suspect and one found at a crime scene, which draws a direct link between the two, suggesting guilt. What is often forgotten by prosecutors, though, is that a DNA "match" is based on probabilities (today it is not unusual to have probabilities ranging into the millions), and does not always provide a positive link between suspect and crime scene.

Say, for example, that a DNA expert testifies in an Australian court that a sample found at the crime scene is 35 million times more likely to come from the defendant than from any other person selected at random from the same population. Given that the population of Australia is currently around 20 million people, this is rather suggestive that this match is highly unlikely to occur with more than one person in the Australian population, and so this sample belongs to this person (and therefore, he or she must be guilty). This ignores the fact that the crime may have been committed by a tourist, or that the probabilities do not exclude any other person, which may be the case when those probabilities are less than the nation's population. The situation is not much different in profiling, and as illustrated on page 154, in New Jersey v Fortin, Roy Hazelwood essentially testified to this very same issue using "signature analysis" instead of DNA.

It is simply not possible for behavioral evidence to meet the threshold of individuation. This means that profiling cannot implicate a person to the exclusion of all others. This is not to say that this very thing has not been tried many times before, as demonstrated in the case studies beginning on page 152.

In another example, a profiler might testify to their conclusions and claim that the suspect on trial "fits" the profile. This may create the following line of reasoning in the mind of the jury:

1 The profile is of the person who committed this crime.
2 The accused is being prosecuted for this crime.
3 The accused fits the profile of the person guilty of this crime.
4 The accused must be guilty of this crime.

Opposite A DNA autoradiogram is produced during DNA analysis. The visible black bands correspond with the four nucleotide bases that make up the genetic sequence. Every individual, with the exception of identical twins, has a unique genetic sequence. DNA recovery and analysis are valuable to cases where forensic evidence is foremost.

Above Forensic expert Dr. Henry Lee points to an evidence chart as he discusses DNA testing at the O.J. Simpson murder trial.

In the absence of other information this flawed line of reasoning is potentially damaging as it suggests the person currently on trial is the party responsible, even before any other information is presented.

PITFALLS IN EXPERT EVIDENCE

Courts worldwide are cautious of new forms of evidence and profiling is no exception. Courts in Australia, America, and the United Kingdom have been reluctant to allow profilers to present their opinion to the court. This is not only because individual profilers sometimes don't meet the standards for expert opinion, but also because of a number of other considerations that run parallel to other discussions of expert evidence. These include prejudice and bias, how complex the evidence is, and the willingness of experts to step outside their area of expertise.

It's useful to look at the results of one particular study that investigated just how much of a problem expert testimony can be. The study took place in Australia but has worldwide relevance.

Expert Evidence Study

Two legal practitioners at the forefront of expert evidence in Australia, Ian Freckleton and Hugh Selby, carried out a study in which 478 magistrates (in Australia, a magistrate is the equivalent of a judge in a lower court) and judges were polled about their opinions on expert evidence. Only a little over half (244) completed the survey. What the researchers found is not only interesting but raises serious concerns about the use of expert evidence.

Because of the requirements raised by rules of expert evidence, a good deal of the evidence given tends to be complex and incomprehensible. Of the 244 responses, 52.8 percent of the judges claim they experienced difficulty in understanding the evidence of experts, and 41.8 percent of the magistrates also had this difficulty.

Of those who said they had trouble understanding the evidence, 77 percent said this happened frequently and 14 percent said this happened occasionally. When ranking the complexity of certain evidence, Freckleton and Selby found that psychiatric evidence, psychological evidence, and scientific evidence were viewed by judges as the most complex. What is most interesting about this is that, depending on the profiler, their evidence comes under one or more of these three types.

In giving their testimony, experts may also use complex or technical language, further muddying the waters. The main concern that arises is that if judges, whose professional lives revolve around the law and evidence, are often confused, what hope does the jury have, a group with no such experience to call on?

Of similar concern is the finding that experts often wander into areas not within their field of expertise, providing testimony that might be incorrect or misleading. Just over three-quarters of those in the survey claimed that experts occasionally went outside of their area of expertise. More alarmingly, 12 percent claimed that this happened frequently.

KEY FINDINGS OF STUDY

1 Most judges experience difficulty understanding expert evidence.

2 Psychiatric, psychological, and scientific evidence are the most complex.

3 Many judges find it difficult to understand technical language used in expert evidence.

4 Experts often wander into areas not within their field of expertise.

5 If one side calls on an expert witness and the other doesn't, the jury may be biased.

THE DEPRAVITY STANDARD

Courts across the world are using terms like "heinous," "atrocious," and "cruel" when weighing penalties for a variety of crimes. However, the interpretations of these terms and resulting punishment vary enormously. In one case the crime might be the destruction of a farmer's crop, in other the indictment might be war crimes. The Depravity Standard, conceived by Michael Welner, M.D., a forensic psychiatrist at New York University School of Medicine, is a research tool that may help juries, judges, and criminal profilers in future trials. It aims to better guide jurors beyond their biases to focus on facts of the case that reflect what exactly happened – as opposed to a defendant's race, socioeconomic background, personality, appearance, media hype, or other aspects of a crime that may unfairly weigh against a defendant's just fate.

While today's crime scene investigators primarily use the forensic sciences to establish suspects' guilt or innocence, this landmark research effort brings together forensic scientists of various disciplines to help courts distinguish the most heinous of violent and non-violent crimes from the norm. The Depravity Standard distinguishes the intents, actions, and attitudes that characterize a crime.

In tomorrow's courts, evidence may be gathered about these features of a crime with the combined input of crime scene investigators, forensic pathologists, forensic anthropologists, forensic psychiatrists and psychologists, neurosurgeons and emergency medicine specialists, and forensic dentists.

Dr. Welner and his colleagues set up a series of research experiments to establish what citizens of different communities and different countries could reach agreement on, for distinguishing the most evil of crimes. That research remains available for public participation (www.depravityscale.org), in order for the Standard to reflect prevailing societal attitudes.

With a Depravity Standard derived from these sources and clear criteria set for each of the over 20 potential features of a depraved crime, investigators now have guidance to educate sentencing courts in trials from computer hacking to war crimes tribunals. For example, anthropologists will probe exhumed bones for signs of "actions that maximize damage;" forensic pathologists will recognize, from hesitation marks, "intent to emotionally traumatize," or "disrespect for the victim after the fact," in signs of sexual contact with a corpse. Forensic psychiatrists will probe the motivation of "exploiting a trusting relationship," in interviews of perpetrators, witnesses, and victims. Forensic dentists will contribute to exploring the possibility of "actions that cause grotesque suffering," while crime scene investigators will help solve questions of the actions "involving others in the criminal enterprise in order to enhance destruction."

Using a Depravity Standard, tomorrow's juries will still be charged – as they are today – with deciding whether a crime is "heinous," "evil," or "vile," for example. In 39 American states, for example, courts use such words to affect sentencing – in matters that include death penalty cases as well. With no standardized guidance, sentencing juries are much more likely to arbitrarily pass sentence; with a Depravity Standard, juries inexperienced in confronting the range of crime and deviant behavior gain a frame of reference to assist them.

As discussed earlier, criminal profiling methodologies do not reliably guarantee that the same profile will be generated by qualified professionals following a given methodology. This lack of inter-rater reliability, which has limited the potential for the admissibility of profiling as expert evidence is carefully addressed in the definitions of evidence and thresholds in items of the Depravity Standard. A qualified, trained professional who adheres to the protocol of the Depravity Standard is therefore likely to arrive at the same determination about a crime (low, medium, or high depravity) as another colleague following the prescribed protocols.

The Depravity Standard may only be applied if evidence exists to support the presence or absence of a given intent, action, or attitude. For example, there can be no consideration of "intent to emotionally traumatize" unless evidence has been gathered that specifically supports it. Inference is therefore minimized, which is good news for profilers and court systems the world over.

TERMS TO LABEL THE CRIMES

Even without the courtroom rhetoric and drama of a trial, the similarities and overlap between the words used to descibe crimes are evident.

- Heinous – grossly wicked or reprehensible; abominable
- Atrocious – extremely evil or cruel; monstrous; exceptionally bad; abominable
- Cruel – disposed to inflict pain or suffering; causing suffering
- Evil – morally bad or wrong; wicked; causing ruin, injury, or pain; harmful; malicious
- Vile – loathsome; disgusting; morally depraved; ignoble or wicked

Bias is a real problem in courts. Because one side has an expert and the other doesn't, this may give the appearance they are more convinced about their case. This may have a biasing effect on the jury. Understandably, the fact that experts are called either by the defense or by prosecution means that the evidence they give will often be favorable to the side that calls them, and "hired guns" such as this are a real problem with expert evidence. In the Freckleton and Selby study, 35 percent of judges claimed that bias is one of the major issues plaguing expert evidence.

The amount of time and money given to either side may also dictate if, how, and when experts are used, which means that it may often be a matter of the best justice you can afford. Many of the judges and magistrates complained about seeing the same expert repeatedly testifying for the same side in a number of different cases, suggesting there may be some devotion to either defense or prosecution work.

CASE STUDIES

Despite the above concerns, there are a number of examples where profiling has been used in court, either directly as profiling or under the veil of some other form of evidence. Occasionally it is hidden in other practices to bypass the rules of evidence, or it may be presented innocently and without any intent to deceive the court. Either way, profiling evidence has been accepted in a number of courts around the world.

The case studies presented below don't always fit neatly into one type of expert evidence, and one case may represent a number of different rules, but they demonstrate the general use of the rules of expert evidence.

New Jersey versus Fortin

Steven Fortin was convicted for the 1994 murder of New Jersey woman Melissa Padilla. Her body, which was lying half inside a sewer, was discovered by her boyfriend. She was wearing a shirt, no bra, and was naked from the waist down. Her shorts, with the underwear still in them, were found on a nearby shrub.

Closer inspection showed several items scattered around the body, including several bags of food, a store receipt, an earring, cigarette butts, and a one-dollar note with blood on it. Another bloodstain was found inside the pipe, and she had been beaten about the head, her face was swollen, and her nose was broken. At the autopsy, it was found that she had been manually strangled and anally assaulted, bitten on the left breast, on the left nipple, and on the left side of her chin.

Less than one year later, Trooper Vicki Gardner pulled over to check a vehicle parked on the side of the road. The driver, Steven Fortin, told her he was having trouble with his vehicle, and Trooper Gardner smelled alcohol on his breath. She called for backup and administered roadside sobriety tests. When she was sealing the tests, Fortin grabbed her by the throat and strangled her until she was semiconscious. While in this state, Fortin sexually assaulted her. As Gardner's backup arrived, Fortin sped off in his own vehicle with Gardner. He punched her in the face and swore at her.

He soon lost control of the car, and after it overturned he ran away, only to be arrested a mile or so away a short time later. Trooper Gardner's face had been severely beaten and her nose was fractured, she had been manually strangled, and during the sexual assault she had been bitten on the left nipple, left breast, and her left chin. Her underpants, pants, and bra had been removed during the sexual assault and when found in the vehicle, her pants still had the underwear inside of them. Fortin plea-bargained to the assault on Gardner.

The Maine State Police contacted the New Jersey police about Fortin. They felt that the New Jersey investigation into the death of Melissa Padilla (which no one had been charged for yet) contained information relevant to Fortin:

1 He lived in the general vicinity of Padilla at the time of the offense.
2 Earlier on the day of the murder Fortin had fought with his girlfriend.
3 Later that day his girlfriend noted scratches on his head, chest, and neck.
4 An examination of the bite marks on Padilla's breasts led to an opinion that they were caused by Fortin while the other bite marks "may" have been caused by him.

INFORMATION RELEVANT TO FORTIN

1 Both crimes were high risk.

2 Both crimes were committed impulsively.

3 Both crimes were committed against female victims.

4 They were both fully mature in age.

5 Both were committed against someone who had crossed their path.

6 Both victims were alone when attacked.

7 Both assaults took place adjacent to or on a well-traveled road.

8 Both attacks occurred during darkness.

9 No weapons were used during the assault.

10 Both victims sustained only blunt force injuries.

11 Both assaults took place at the point of confrontation.

12 Both victims sustained trauma primarily to the upper face with no damage to the teeth.

13 Both victims had their lower garments totally removed.

14 Both victims were wearing shorts but their breasts were free.

15 Neither victim had seminal fluid on or in her body.

In an attempt to make sense of the behavioral evidence, the State sought expert testimony from Roy Hazelwood, an expert on violent crime who had spent much of his professional career with the FBI as a criminal profiler. In reviewing the material relevant to both crimes, Hazelwood concluded that the MO of the crimes demonstrated 15 consistent aspects. These aspects are found in the table above.

In his testimony, Hazelwood noted that he had never in his 35 years of law enforcement experience or some 7,000 cases seen this particular constellation of MO behaviors. In addition to the MO elements present, his report went on to discuss five "ritual" or signature aspects, which he claimed also linked the crimes. These were:

1 Bites to the lower chin
2 Bites to the lateral left breast
3 Injurious anal penetration
4 Brutal facial beating
5 Manual (frontal) strangulation

Once again, Hazelwood testified that he had never seen this particular constellation of ritual behaviors, giving further strength to his

opinion that one man was responsible for both attacks. Using "linkage analysis" he determined that "the likelihood of different offenders committing two such extremely unique crimes was highly improbable."

While much of the testimony was allowed in the original trial, the Appellate Division decided that the linkage analysis was not reliable enough to be admitted as evidence. The testimony spoke to the "ultimate issue," which is the role of the jury to determine. Because Fortin had admitted to the Gardner offense, and because the MO and signature elements of both crimes suggested the same offender, then it could be argued that Fortin also committed the Padilla crime.

The Supreme Court of New Jersey agreed that the testimony of this expert profiler should not reach the jury, adding that expert evidence needs to meet three thresholds. The first is that the expertise must be outside of the experience of the average person. Secondly, that the field in question must be at a level where an expert's opinion will be sufficiently reliable, and lastly, that the expert must have adequate

Above Defense files on the first day of the trial of three French photographers, in October 2003. The photographers stood accused of chasing the car transporting Princess Diana and Dodi al-Fayed on the night of their fatal car crash in Paris.

expertise in the field. The issue was not so much whether Hazelwood had the relevant expertise but whether he could present his testimony to the jury. In line with this, the Court accepted that he could testify as an expert and could discuss the similarities between crimes. He could not, however, go beyond this into conclusions of guilt or innocence.

Because of the nature of his testimony, Hazelwood has been criticized not only for the way his testimony suggested Fortin's guilt, but also because he attempted to use behavioral evidence as individuating evidence (see chapter 4). The Supreme Court granted an appeal to Fortin on the grounds that the trial court committed a reversible error in permitting Hazelwood to testify without the submission of a reliable database. They further decided that Hazelwood was not an expert in the areas he testified in and that he should not have been allowed to give the testimony he gave.

The Queen versus Ranger

The decision in Ranger is of great interest to the profiling community because it helped establish precedent relevant to profiling evidence in a number of jurisdictions. In this case, a police officer from the Behavioral Science Section was admitted as an expert in staging. The facts of the case follow.

Rohan Ranger was accused of the first degree murder of his former girlfriend Marsha Ottey and the manslaughter of her sister, Tamara. Ranger had been in a relationship with Marsha and had not been able to accept the breakup of the relationship. Both of the deaths occurred at roughly the same time, and both bodies were found in the house they shared with their mother. It was alleged that the accused and his cousin, Adrian Kincaid, had stabbed and killed the two girls. Although the house had the appearance of being ransacked, only three items had been taken. All items belonged to Marsha. One of them, a necklace, was given to her by Rohan Ranger.

The profile offered as evidence related to the crime scene and to the presence of "staging." Specifically, that someone had staged a break and enter in order to divert attention away from their connection to the victims. Following an initial inquiry regarding the admissibility of the evidence, the trial judge ruled: "I am satisfied that opinion evidence is needed in this case" since it would provide information outside of the experience and knowledge of the jury, and judging whether a break and entry is authentic or staged is also not likely to be within their experience. To be able to offer this evidence though, the prosecution had to provide an expert in this particular area.

The expert witness relied on by the Crown was Detective Inspector Kathryn Lines from the Ontario Provincial Police who claimed she had considerable experience in the area of behavioral profiling. The prosecution confirmed that the Detective Inspector's evidence was being offered as "an expert witness in the area of staged crime scenes" who could confirm that this crime had in fact been staged. Neither side made a submission regarding the qualifications of the expert in the area in which she testified, and the trial judge ruled that she was qualified to give the evidence. During the initial inquiry into the proposed testimony, Detective Inspector Lines conceded there was no independent and objective process against which to test the theory of a staged crime scene.

The defense was concerned that the evidence might wander into the area of Ranger's motive in the crime, but was assured this was not the intention of the evidence. Unfortunately, the prosecution was able to draw out the Detective Inspector's opinion about motive at least three times, also providing what she felt were some of the offender's characteristics (a profile). Each time, the defense counsel objected to the expert's opinion because it went beyond the agreed boundaries of admissible evidence (and would probably have had a prejudicial effect on the jury), and each time the defense was overruled (which allowed the questions and answers to have an impact on the jurors' decisions).

The first line of questioning levelled at the profiler was that the evidence suggested that the offender was more interested in Marsha as a victim than they were in Tamara. Despite an objection that this had more to do with the offender's psychology than the staging of the crime scene, the question was allowed and the expert answered that the offender did have more of an interest in Marsha.

The second question related to the type of person who was likely to stage a crime scene and the expert was allowed to provide commentary from a crime scene manual that "it is always someone who had some kind of association or relationship with the victim."

The defense raised the objection that this opinion was "dime store psychology" which placed Ranger squarely within the frame as the type

of person likely to commit the crime. Detective Inspector Lines was also allowed to testify that only items belonging to Marsha were missing from the crime scene, which suggested that the offender had "a particular interest in the possessions or things related to her."

When the defense cross-examined the expert, three of their questions were related to the degree to which her opinion had been influenced by her knowledge of the outcome the police were hoping for (she was, remember, a police officer herself). The trial judge brought this line of questioning to a halt, reminding the jury that it was their opinion which was important, and not that of the expert or the police.

Later, the Court of Appeal held that the defense should have been allowed to continue with that line of inquiry. In offering their opinion on the matter, they referenced a previous decision from the case of Guy Paul Morin, also from Canada, that "profiling, once a suspect has been identified, can be misleading and dangerous, as the investigators' summary of the relevant facts may be colored by their suspicions."

The Ontario Court of Appeal rejected the evidence of the expert in this case because Line's "opinions amounted to no more than educated guesses" and because of this, the criminal profiling evidence was inadmissible.

The Estate of Samuel Sheppard v The State of Ohio
With a civil case being brought against the state of Ohio by the family of Dr. Samuel Sheppard, the state contracted Gregg O. McCrary, a former profiler with the FBI, to conduct a profile of the likely suspect. Again, the central issue for which the profile was sought was the belief that the crime scene had been staged, and it was assumed McCrary's evidence would be able to bring out this information in a way that might prove valuable to an understanding of the basic facts of the case.

Marilyn Reece Sheppard was found dead in the master bedroom of her home on July 4, 1954. She had been beaten around the head approximately 25 to 35 times. She was wearing her pajama top, which

Opposite The body of Marilyn Sheppard as found at the crime scene on July 4, 1954. The profiler on this case, Gregg O. McCrary, concluded from the position of the body that this was a secondary scene and the body had been arranged to suggest a sexually motivated attack.

had been pushed up to expose her breasts, one leg of her trousers had been pulled down, and her legs were hanging over the end of the bed – one either side of the bed post.

From this, McCrary concluded the crime had been staged to give the appearance that the murder was in fact sexually motivated. The basis of this conclusion was that there was evidence of overkill (more force or violence than is necessary simply to complete the crime, which is usually suggestive of anger toward the victim) inferring that the offender and the victim may have known one another.

While there was a great deal of rage in the way the victim was killed, it appeared that a level of care had been taken in removing the pajama pants; they were not ripped or torn in any way. These two things were contradictory. Because of this, it was suggested there was no physical or behavioral evidence to infer that the crime was in fact sexually motivated, so it must have been staged to give it the appearance that it was. The care with which the body of the victim was placed also indicated to McCrary that the offender had spent a considerable time at the crime scene. This was odd because typically offenders spend no more time than necessary there. The arrangement of the crime scene suggested to McCrary that the offender may have had a legitimate reason for being at the scene and was not worried about being interrupted or discovered.

In other parts of the house there was evidence of ransacking, including the drawers of Sam Sheppard's desk, his medical bag, and trophies – although the damage was minimal. The only things taken were some money from his wallet and some morphine from his medical bag: but this was based on Sheppard's own account. His police badge (he was a police volunteer) was left untouched. Given the absence of damage to the property and the fact that only a few small items were taken, McCrary argued that this too had been staged. Other

---

Opposite Dr. Samuel Sheppard (center), whose story inspired the popular television series and the film *The Fugitive*, starring Harrison Ford. Proceedings began in January 2000 in the wrongful imprisonment suit against the State of Ohio filed by Sheppard's son, Samuel Reese Sheppard Jr., DNA evidence, some previously unused, was essential to this trial; however, Samuel's crusade to overturn the initial ruling failed.

inconsistencies deemed to be of importance were evidence of overkill with the victim, but relatively unscathed property. This, along with the length of time that the offender spent at the scene, further suggested that whoever did this had continued interest in the house.

Despite Dr. Sheppard's claim that the killer touched him when removing his wristwatch and ring, there was no blood found on him at all, except for some small amounts on the watch when it was recovered outside the property. Given the level of violence in the homicide, the killer would have been covered in a considerable amount of blood, and Dr. Sheppard did not, by his own account, clean himself up at all.

Furthermore, there was no blood on his trousers, even though it was claimed that the killer removed Sheppard's wallet from his pocket, and Sheppard claimed to have felt for his wife's pulse: this would no doubt have resulted in blood transfer from his wife to him.

As the crime would have taken time to commit, McCrary proposed that the offender had a legitimate reason for being at the scene and was not concerned about being interrupted. This indicated that the person was not only familiar with the scene, but felt comfortable being there.

Later, McCrary went on to match every aspect of the crime to a Staged Domestic Homicide, discussed in the *Crime Classification Manual* and then concluded:

" The totality of the physical, forensic, and behavioral evidence allows for only one logical conclusion and that is that the homicide of Marilyn Reese Sheppard on July 4, 1956 was a staged domestic homicide committed by Dr. Sheppard. The known indicators of criminal staging as well as the known crime scene indicators consistent with a staged domestic homicide are abundantly present. This evidence not only supports no other logical conclusion, but also significantly contradicts Dr. Samuel Sheppard's testimony and statements. "

After a lengthy initial inquiry into McCrary's evidence, it was decided that it should be limited to discussing staging in general, and not specifically to the Sheppard case. This was largely due to an affidavit provided by Brent Turvey who also noted that the determinations were made largely from those characteristics of a Staged Domestic Homicide in the *Crime Classification Manual*, and that while

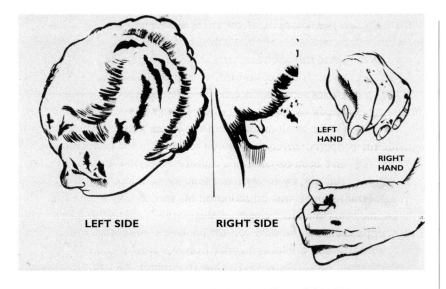

this may be considered by some to be a useful investigative guide, it is not suited to addressing legal issues in a court of law.

Most importantly, McCrary went as far in his analysis as to name the accused, speaking directly to the ultimate issue and cementing Sheppard's guilt, the prejudicial value of which cannot even be measured. McCrary admitted having no experience in investigating domestic homicides or interpreting blood splatters, making his conclusions on these issues outside his area of expertise. Beyond the considerable questions these issues of his testimony raise, it would appear that the basic facts of the case were not even fully examined. For example, at one point Dr. Sheppard claimed he was unconscious on the beach, but that he regained consciousness in the bedroom (which is a fairly significant contradiction). This would seem to support Turvey's claims that the fundamental evidence was not rigorously examined before his conclusions were drawn and opinions given to the court.

In the end, the jury decided for the State of Ohio. The judge ruled that McCrary could not give evidence relating to staging in the Sheppard case, but that he would be allowed to testify to staging in general. Ultimately, the court held that his opinions were not sufficiently reliable, but that he would be allowed to give an expert opinion on the case.

CONCLUSION

Through the examination of academic and mainstream literature, court transcripts, and independent adjudications, I have attempted to offer in this book a history and analysis of the ever-growing discipline of criminal profiling. From the outset it has been my goal not to portray profiling as something it is not, but to present a "warts and all" account of the past and current state of play in the field, and to provide a more critical account than other material on the same subject.

The field of criminal profiling is still quite new and we have a lot to learn. Our understanding of some parts of the process is somewhat naïve, while our understanding of other areas is more developed. It is only through further research and exploration into the different types of profiling and the cases in which they are applied that we come to a better understanding of the variety of ways profiling can assist the police with their inquiries.

For reasons of brevity, there is a number of areas significant to the field of criminal profiling that I have not been able to include in this book. For example, to date there are no universal education or training standards through which one can aspire to become a criminal profiler. A whole other work could be dedicated to the theoretical and practical background to criminal profiling and the variety of ways that one might develop one's skills to become a profiling professional. Also, while there is a number of groups involved in setting standards for profilers (such as the Association of Chief Police Officers and the Academy of Behavioral Profiling), each group can ostensibly only set rules and regulations for their own members. Individual practitioners are therefore free to do whatever they please without regard for ethics or professionalism.

Even though this book has been critical of some aspects of profiling, and by extension the behavior of some profilers, I am an advocate of profiling and extremely hopeful that the field will progress in leaps and bounds in the years to come. My experience with police and private individuals who seek out a profile is that exposure even to true-crime material and media-based fictional accounts is making consumers more aware of what profiling can do and the ways it might assist them in their efforts. This can be a very good thing. Not only this, but the awareness of different methods and what each has to offer will also grow over time.

It is my opinion that one of the reasons the field of criminal profiling hasn't advanced further than it has (when we have had more than enough potential to do so) is because a number of groups and individuals have a vested interest in keeping the field where it is. This gives them carte blanche over the field and the "right" to practice it and teach it as they wish. This, I believe, is not conducive to advancing the field and, in fact, does it a disservice.

I have also found in the profession a reluctance among many to be critical of those things that have been done incorrectly, or those that have caused harm. As readers can see here plainly, profiling is far from perfect. There are a great many instances in which either the profiles or the profilers themselves have caused varying degrees of harm. We should not be afraid to point this out and we should definitely not fear reprisal. As discussed by Keith Inmand and Norah Rudin in their excellent book, *Principles and Practice of Criminalistics: The Profession of Forensic Science*, the best way to ensure ethical practice is by exercising peer pressure.

The fascinating if somewhat tumultuous history and development of the field of criminal profiling has set the stage for the current state of affairs. With a history like this, the future of profiling promises to be something very exciting indeed.

Wayne Petherick

GLOSSARY

ambusher: under Rossmo's geographic profiling, an ambusher attacks victims only in areas where they have a lot of control, such as a home or workplace

analysis: a method of criminal profiling relying on deductive logic.

anger excitation: a motivation in which the offender gets sexual satisfaction from the pain and suffering of the victim. Otherwise referred to as a sadist

anger retaliatory: a motivation in which the offender acts out as the result of anger arising from real or imagined wrongs. The victims of these offenses may be individuals, groups, or an organization

area of expertise rule: a rule of expert evidence stating that the area in which the expert is testifying must be an established or recognized field where others can evaluate its theories and application

ballistics: the field of firearms examination

Behavioral Evidence Analysis (BEA): a method of criminal profiling relying on deductive logic

commuter: an offender who moves out from their base into a different area in which they offend

class evidence: general characteristics that separate groups of items from other groups of dissimilar items

common knowledge rule: a rule of expert testimony stating that the expert should not be called when the matter under consideration is within the experience or knowledge of the jury

Criminal Investigative Analysis (CIA): a method of profiling developed by the FBI which relies on statistical generalizations

criminal profile: the inference of personality and behavioral characteristics from the evidence of the crime

Daubert rule: a rule of expert evidence in the US which gave judges more discretion in the evidence allowed into their courtroom. It revolves around whether theories can be tested, whether they have been peer-reviewed, their error rate, standards, and acceptance

deduction: a type of logic in which the conclusion must be true if the information on which it is based is true

Diagnostic Evaluation (DE): a generic name for the profiles done by mental health professionals

disorganized offender: a type of offender in the FBI method who exhibits little planning, leaves lots of evidence and is occasionally mentally ill

distance decay: a geospatial behavior theory suggesting that crimes become fewer the further from home an offender travels

Dragnet: a geographic profiling computer program developed by psychologists at the University of Liverpool

equivocal forensic analysis: the first stage of the Behavioral Evidence Analysis model in which the nature of all physical evidence is examined

expertise rule: a rule of expert evidence stating that an expert must be an expert in their respective area

factual basis rule: a rule of expert evidence stating that there must be some factual basis for the evidence they present

forensic awareness: the knowledge of police and investigative tactics and procedures that an offender evidences in their behavior

Frye rule: a rule of expert evidence revolving around whether something is generally accepted in its scientific community

geographic profiling: an inductive profiling method that attempts to identify the likely residential base of an offender based on their crime sites

hunter: an offense style where a victim is sought out in the offender's home area

incident risk: the risk present at the moment an offender acquires a victim

individuating evidence: evidence that indicates the source of a sample or object to the exclusion of all others

induction: a form of reasoning involving statistical generalization from past research and experience

interpersonal coherence: the way in which people adopt a style of dealing with others in their interpersonal relationships, where criminal behavior will essentially be a reflection of non-criminal behavior

Investigative Psychology (IP): an inductive profiling method developed by David Canter in the UK which employs complex statistical methods to develop theories

least effort principle: theory that, when given two similar options, most people will choose the one requiring least effort

leptosome: someone with a thin, athletic build

lifestyle risk: the overall risk present to someone based on their personality, personal, professional, and social environments

linkage blindness: the failure of law enforcement to successfully link serial crimes of the same offender

Locard's exchange principle: the idea that when an offender enters a crime scene, they both take something of that scene away with them and leave something of themselves behind

marauder: an offender who strikes out from and returns to a central location

medical examiner: a doctor who performs examinations of the cause, manner, and mechanism of death

modus operandi: those things an offender does which are necessary for the successful completion of the offense

motive: the force that impels an offender to the criminal act

organized offender: a type of offender in the FBI method who exhibits careful planning, leaves little evidence and may be psychopathic

poacher: an offense style where the offender travels away from home to find victims

power assertive: an offender who is motivated by a sense of personal inadequacy manifested in power, control and domination over victims

power reassurance: an offender who is motivated by a sense of personal inadequacy where they act out as though there is a personal relationship between them and the victim.

precautionary act: an act intended to assist an offender in escaping capture either before, during, or after the offense.

premise: that information on which a conclusion is based

profiler's opening caveat: any exceptions that a profiler provides as to the accuracy or utility of their reports

profiling inputs: any information on which a profile is based

psychopathic: a personality disorder whereby those afflicted have a callous disregard for the rights and welfare of others

psychotic: a state of altered reality, usually the result of a mental illness

pyknic: someone of a short, stocky stature with a rounded abdomen

raptor: an offender who attacks a victim immediately upon encountering them

risk assessment: the determination of the amount of risk present to a victim or offender before, during or after the commission of an offense

scientific method: a systematic process of obtaining knowledge through the process of collecting and interpreting evidence

sexual homicide: a homicide involving sexual acts against the victim

signature behavior: specific component behaviors that were not necessary for the successful completion of the offense

signature aspect: the overall theme of the offense as indicated by the signature behaviors

somatotype: body type

spatial mean: the average distance between all crime sites

staging: deliberate and purposeful alteration of the physical evidence

stalker: an obsessional follower

statistical reliability: the degree to which a result is reproducible over multiple testings

statistical validity: whether a test actually measures what it intends to measure

trapper: an offender who creates a situation where they can draw the victim in

troller: an offender who takes advantage of an opportunistic encounter with a victim during the course of other activities

ultimate issue rule: a rule of evidence which states that an expert must not testify to the guilt or innocence of an individual

ViCAP: the Violent Criminal Apprehension Program. A computer-based crime-linkage system working from information input by analysts based on past and open cases

ViCLAS: the Violent Crime Linkage and Analysis System. A computer-based crime-linkage system working from information input by analysts based on past and open cases

victimology: a thorough and comprehensive examination of the victim of a crime

BIBLIOGRAPHY

Ainsworth, P. (2001). *Offender profiling and crime analysis*. Devon: Willan Publishing.

Boon, J.C.W. (1997). "The contribution of personality theories to psychological profiling" in Jackson, J., & Bekerian, D. (1997). (eds.) *Offender profiling: Theory research and practice*. Chichester: Wiley.

Brussel, J.A. (1968). *Casebook of a crime psychiatrist*. New York: Dell Publishing.

Burgess, A.W., & Hazelwood, R.R. (1995). (eds.) *Practical aspects of rape investigation: A multidisciplinary approach*. Boca Raton: CRC Press.

Burgess, A.W., & Ressler, R.K. (1985). "Sexual homicide crime scenes and patterns of criminal behavior." *National Institute of Justice Grant 82-IJ-CX-0065*.

Canter, D. (1995). *Criminal shadows: Inside the mind of the serial killer*. London: HarperCollins.

Canter, D. (2003). *Mapping murder: The secrets of geographic profiling*. London: Virgin Books.

Canter, D. & Larkin, P. (1993). "The environmental range of serial rapists." *Journal of Environmental Psychology*, 13, pp. 63–69.

Conan-Doyle, A. (1964). *The sign of four*. London: Jonathan Cape.

Daily Mirror, September 15, 1994.

Daubert v Merrell Dow Pharmaceuticals, Inc. (1993). 113 S. Ct. 2786

Douglas, J.E., & Munn, C.M. (1992). "Violent crime scene analysis: Modus operandi, signature and staging." *FBI Law Enforcement Bulletin, February*.

Douglas, J.E., & Olshaker, M. (1996). *Mindhunter: Inside the elite FBI elite serial crime unit*. London: Mandarin.

Edwards, C. (1998). "Behavior and the law reconsidered: psychological syndromes and profiles." *Journal of Forensic Sciences, 43 (1)*, pp. 141–150.

Egger, S.A. (2004). *The killers among us: An examination of serial murder and its investigation*. (second ed.). New Jersey: Prentice Hall.

Eggleston, R. (1983). *Evidence: Proof and probability*. (second ed.). London: Weidenfeld and Nicholson.

Federal Bureau of Investigation. *FBI profile of serial killer*. Available from http://www.brgov.com/taskforce/victimprofile.htm

Field, D. (2003). *Criminal profiling: Some legal perspectives*. Bond University: unpublished manuscript.

The Forensic Examiner. (2002). "Falsely accused? Who is the Boston strangler?" January/February edition.

Freckelton, I., & Selby, H. (1999). *Australian judicial attitudes towards expert evidence*. Australian Institute of Judicial Administration.

Freckelton, I., & Selby, H. (2001). *Australian magistrates' attitudes towards expert evidence: A comparative study*. Australian Institute of Judicial Administration.

Geberth, V.J. (1996). *Practical homicide investigation: Tactics, procedures and forensic techniques* (third ed.). Boca Raton: CRC Press.

Gross, H. (1924). *Criminal investigation: A practical textbook for magistrates, police officers and lawyers.* London: Sweet and Maxwell.

Groth, A.N. (1979). *Men who rape: The psychology of the offender.* New York: Plenum Press.

Gudjonsson, G., & Copson, G. (1997). "The role of the expert in criminal investigation" in Jackson, J., & Bekerian, D. (1997). *Offender profiling: Theory, research and practice.* Chichester: Wiley.

Hancock, L. (2000). "FBI mislead Reno to get tear-gas OK, ex-agent alleged. Request to use force in Waco omitted expert's caution." *Dallas News.*

Holmes, R.M., & Holmes, S.T. (2002). *Profiling violent crimes: An investigative tool.* Thousand Oaks: Sage Publications.

Hudson, D., & Hills, B. (1999). *An hour to kill: A true story of love, murder and justice in a small Southern town.* Tampa: McGregor Publishing.

Ihle, B. (2002). *Expert evidence: Purposes and pitfalls.* Bond University: unpublished manuscript.

Investigations Subcommittee and Defense Policy Panel of the Committee on Armed Services House of Representatives (1990). *USS Iowa tragedy: An investigative failure.* Washington: US Government Printing Office.

Johnston, W.W. (1999). Memo to the Attorney General of the United States. US Department of Justice.

Kirk, R. (1974). *Crime investigation.* (second ed.). New York: John Wiley & Sons.

Kocsis, R.N., & Hayes, A.F. (2004). "Believing is seeing? Investigating the perceived accuracy of criminal psychological profiles." *International Journal of Offender Therapy and Comparative Criminology, 48(2)*, pp. 149–160.

Kocsis, R.N., & Heller, G.Z. (2004). "Believing is seeing II: Beliefs and perceptions of criminal psychological profiles." *International Journal of Offender Therapy and Comparative Criminology, 48(3)*, pp. 313–329.

Kocsis, R.N., & Middeldorp, J. (2004). "Believing is seeing III: Perceptions of content in criminal psychological profiles." *International Journal of Offender Therapy and Comparative Criminology, 48(4)*, pp. 477–494.

Lucas, D.M. (2003). "Highlights in the forensic science odyssey: The first ten thousand years." Presentation to the American Society of Crime Lab Directors.

McCrary, G. (1999). Criminal investigative analysis in The Estate of Samuel Sheppard v The State of Ohio. Available from http://www.courttv.com/archive/national/2000/0131/mccrary_ctv.html

McGrath, M. (2001). "Signature in the courtroom: Whose crime is it anyway?" *Journal of Behavioral Profiling, 2 (2).*

McGrath, M. G. (2000). "Criminal profiling: Is there a role for the forensic psychiatrist?" *Journal of the American Academy of Psychiatry and Law, 28*, pp. 315–324.

New Jersey v Fortin (2000). 162 N.J 517, 745 A.2d 509

Petherick, W.A. (2003). "Criminal profiling: What's in a name?" *Journal of Law and Social Challenges*, June.

Petherick, W.A. (2002). "The fallacy of accuracy in criminal profiling." *The Journal of Behavioral Profiling, 3 (1)*.

Pinizzotto, A.J., & Finkel, N. (1990). "Criminal personality profiling: An outcome and process study." *Law and Human Behavior, 14*, pp. 215–233.

Popper, K. (2003). *The logic of scientific discovery*. London: Routledge Classics.

Poythress, N., Otto, R.K., Darkes, J., & Starr, L. (1993). "APA's expert panel in the Congressional review of the USS Iowa incident." *The Psychologist, 48 (1)*, pp. 8–15.

Ressler, R.K., Burgess, A.W., & Douglas, J.E. (1988). *Sexual homicides: Patterns and motives*. New York: Lexington Books.

Ressler, R.K., & Shachtman, T. (1992). *Whoever fights monsters: The brilliant FBI detective behind the silence of the lambs*. New York: Pocket Books.

Rossmo, D.K. (2000). *Geographic profiling*. Boca Raton: CRC Press.

R v Ranger (2003). 178 C.C.C. (3d) 375 (Ont. CA).

Saferstein, R. (2004). *Criminalistics: An introduction to forensic science*. New Jersey: Prentice Hall.

Thompson, C.C. (1999). *A Glimpse of Hell: The explosion on the USS Iowa and its cover up*. New York: W.W. Norton & Co.

Turvey, B.E. (2000). "Modus operandi." *Encyclopedia of Forensic Science*. London: Academic Press.

Turvey, B.E. (2002). *Criminal profiling: An introduction to behavioral evidence analysis*. (second ed.). London: Academic Press.

Van Koppen, P.J., & Keijser, J.W. (1997). "Desisting distance decay: On the aggregation of individual crime trips." *Criminology*, August, pp. 505–515.

Wilson, P., & Soothill, K. (1996). "Psychological profiling: Red, green or amber?" *The Police Journal*, July.

Wilson, P., Lincoln, R., & Kocsis, R. (1997). "Validity, utility and ethics of profiling for serial violent and sexual offenders." *Psychiatry, psychology and law, 4 (1)*, pp. 1–12.

Worden, A. (1999). "New allegations: Top officials didn't get full information." *Associated Press*, September 3.

Zonderman, J. (1999). *Beyond the crime lab: The new science of investigation*. New York: John Wiley & Sons.

INDEX

ACKNOWLEDGEMENTS

The publishers and author would like to thank the following for their kind contributions:

Val McDermid for her generous contribution of a foreword.

Dr. Michael McGrath, forensic psychiatrist with the Department of Psychiatry & Behavioral Health at Unity Health System, Rochester, New York.

Dr. Kim Rossmo, Research Professor in the Department of Criminal Justice at Texas State University, and Philip MacLaren from ECRI (Environmental Criminology Research Inc.) for providing images to illustrate the process of geographic profiling.

Brent Turvey, forensic scientist, criminal profiler, and lecturer at Bond University, Australia, for providing case notes from the Louis Peoples serial homicide case and the West Memphis Three triple homicide.

Dr. Michael Welner, a forensic psychiatrist at New York University School of Medicine and chair of The Forensic Panel, for providing information about the Depravity Standard.